net (4.00) 1.5

SO-EKS-945

BIRDS OF THE PLAINS

BIRDS OF THE PLAINS

BY DOUGLAS DEWAR, F.Z.S., I.C.S.
WITH SIXTEEN ILLUSTRATIONS
FROM PHOTOGRAPHS OF LIVING BIRDS
BY CAPTAIN F. D. S. FAYRER, I.M.S.

LONDON : JOHN LANE THE BODLEY HEAD
NEW YORK : JOHN LANE COMPANY MCMIX

WILLIAM BRENDON AND SON, LTD., PRINTERS, PLYMOUTH

PREFACE

IT is easy enough to write a book. The difficulty is to sell the production when it is finished. That, however, is not the author's business. Nevertheless, the labours of the writer are not over when he has completed the last paragraph of his book. He has, then, in most cases, to find a title for it.

This, I maintain, should be a matter of little difficulty. I regard a title as a mere distinguishing mark, a brand, a label, a something by which the book may be called when spoken of—nothing more.

According to this view, the value of a title lies, not in its appropriateness to the subject-matter, but in its distinctiveness.

To illustrate: some years ago a lady entered a bookseller's shop and asked for " Drummond's latest book— *Nux Vomica*." The bookseller without a word handed her *Lux Mundi*.

To my way of thinking *Lux Mundi* is a good title inasmuch as no other popular book has one like it. So distinctive is it that even when different words were substituted the bookseller at once knew what was intended. That the view here put forward does not find favour with the critics may perhaps be inferred by the exception many of them took to the title of my last book—*Bombay Ducks*.

While commending my view to their consideration, I have on this occasion endeavoured to meet them by resorting to a more orthodox designation. I am, doubtless, pursuing a risky policy. Most of the reviewers were kind enough to say that *Bombay Ducks* was a good book with a bad title. When criticising the present work they may reverse the adjectives. Who knows?

D. D.

CONTENTS

ILLUSTRATIONS

BIRDS OF THE PLAINS

BIRDS OF THE PLAINS

BRITISH BIRDS IN THE PLAINS OF INDIA

MOST birds are cosmopolitans and belong to no nationality. Strictly speaking, there is only one British bird, only one bird found in the British Isles and nowhere else, and that is the red grouse (*Tetrao scoticus*).

For this reason some apology seems necessary for the heading of this article. "Birds common to the Plains of India and the British Isles" would doubtless be a more correct title. However, I write as an Englishman. When I meet in a foreign land a bird I knew in England I like to set that bird down as a fellow-countryman.

In India most of the familiar birds: the thrush, the blackbird, the robin redbreast, the wren, the chaffinch, and the blue tit are conspicuous by their absence; their places being taken by such strange forms as *mynas*, *bulbuls*, seven sisters, parakeets, etc. The Englishman is therefore prone to exaggerate the differences between the avifauna of his own country and that of India. The

B

dissimilarity is indeed great, but not so great as is generally supposed.

A complete list of British birds comprises some four hundred species; of these nearly one-half occur in India. But a list of British species is apt to be a misleading document. You may keep a sharp look-out in England for a lifetime without ever setting eyes on many of the so-called British birds. Every feathered thing that has been blown by contrary winds, or whose dead body has been washed by the waves, on to the shores of Albion has been appropriated as a British species. This sounds very hospitable. Unfortunately the hospitality is of a dubious nature, seeing that every casual bird visitor promptly falls a victim to the gun of some self-styled naturalist. Having slaughtered his "feathered friend" the aforesaid naturalist proceeds to boast in the press of his exploit.

I do not deem it correct to speak of these occasional visitors as British birds. On the other hand, I think we may legitimately call the birds we see constantly in England, at certain or all seasons of the year, English birds. Of these many are also found in India. More of them occur in the Punjab than in any other part of the country because of our long cold weather, and because, as the crow flies, if not as the *sahib* travels, the Punjab is nearer England than is any other province.

The ubiquitous sparrow first demands our attention. This much-abused little bird is, thanks to his "push," quite as much at home in the "Gorgeous East" as he is in England. He is certainly not quite so abundant out here; the crows and spotted owlets take care of that. They are very fond of sparrow for breakfast. Nevertheless, *Passer domesticus* is quite plentiful enough and is ever ready to nest inside one's bungalow.

The Indian cock sparrow differs slightly in appearance from the English bird, having more white on the sides of his neck. This is not, as might be supposed, due to the fact that he is not coated with soot to such an extent as the cockney bird. Every widely distributed species, including man, has its local peculiarities, due to climatic influences, isolation, and other causes. If the isolation be maintained long enough the process of divergence continues until the various races differ from one another to such an extent as to be called species. Local races are incipient species, species in the making. The barn owl (*Strix flammea*) is another case in point. This is a familiar owl in England, and is common out here, but not nearly so abundant as the little spotted owlet that makes night hideous by its caterwaulings. The Indian barn owl, which, in default of barns, haunts mosques, temples, deserted buildings, and even secluded verandahs, differs from our English friend in having stronger claws and feet, and the breast spotted instead of plain white. These trivial differences are not usually considered sufficient to justify the division of the barn owl into two species.

Some of our English birds assume diminutive proportions in India, as, for example, the kingfisher and the raven. This may perhaps be attributed to the enervating Indian climate. The common kingfisher (*Alcedo ispida*) is exceedingly common in all parts of India except the Punjab. It does, indeed, occur in that province, but not abundantly. The commonest kingfisher in the Land of the Five Rivers is the much more splendid white-breasted species (*Halcyon smyrnensis*), which may be recognised by its beautiful blue wings with a white bar, and by its anything but melodious "rattling scream."

This winter the ravens are invading Lahore in very large numbers. It is impossible not to notice the great black creatures as they fly overhead in couples or in companies of six or eight, uttering solemn croaks.

But the Indian raven, large as it is, is a diminutive form; its length is but twenty-four inches as compared with the twenty-eight of its English cousin. Moreover, there are slight anatomical differences between the two races; hence the Indian bird was at one time considered to be a separate species and was called *Corvus lawrencii*. There certainly does seem to be some justification for this procedure, since the Indian raven has not the solitary, shy, and retiring disposition of the bird at Home. It consorts with those feathered villains the Indian crows, and, like them, thieves from man and delights to tease and annoy birds bigger than itself by pulling their tail! But there exist ravens of all sizes intermediate between the large European form and the small Indian one, so that it is not possible to find a point at which a line may be drawn between them. For this reason the Indian raven is now held to be one and the same species as the English bird—*Corvus corax*.

Two cousins of the raven, namely, the rook and the jackdaw, also occur in the Punjab. They both visit us in the cold weather and fraternise with the common

THE WHITE-BREASTED KINGFISHER. (HALCYON SMYRNENSIS)

crows. The rook may be readily distinguished from these by the bare whitish patch of skin in front of its face. Last year hundreds of rooks were to be seen in the fields between the big and the little Ravi. They are not so abundant this winter owing to the comparative mildness of the weather.

The jackdaw is very like *Corvus splendens* in appearance. It may, however, be easily distinguished by its white eye. There is at present a jackdaw in confinement in the Lahore "Zoo."

The coot (*Fulica atra*) is another bird common at Home which is also abundant in India. He needs no description, being familiar—too familiar—to every sportsman in India. He is the "black duck" of Thomas Atkins that remains on the *jhil* after all the duck have disappeared. It is unnecessary to say that the bird is not a duck, but a water-hen that apes the manners of one. His black plumage, white face, and the difficulty he experiences in rising from the water prevent him being confounded with a duck.

Ornithological text-books tell us that the skylark (*Alauda arvensis*) visits India during the winter. This may be so, but I do not think I have ever seen one in the Punjab. I have seen thousands of the Indian skylark (*Alauda gulgula*)—a very similar bird, which is said to soar and sing "just as the lark in England does."

As a rule it soars only at daybreak. There are in India so many birds of prey, ever on the look out for quarry, that our larks are not able to sing with impunity at heaven's gate. They usually put forth their vocal efforts from a less exalted platform.

" The eel's foe, the heron " (*Ardea cinerea*), need not
detain us long, although he is a common bird in
both England and India, for the Punjab is too dry to
be a favourite resort of waders. There is, however, a
heron in the "Zoo" at Lahore who lives happily enough
among the ducks and storks in spite of the way in
which the kites worry him when he is at supper.

The blue-rock pigeon (*Columba livia*) is another
English bird found in the Punjab. This must not
be confounded with its cousin (*Columba intermedia*) the
very common Indian blue pigeon, of which so many
have taken up their quarters in the Montgomery Hall.
The European form is not nearly so abundant, and is
distinguished by its paler colour and by the fact that its
lower back is white instead of bluish grey.

The family of birds of prey affords us a large number
of species common to England and India. Almost all
the well-known English raptores are found in India
—the peregrine falcon, the marsh harrier, the hen-
harrier, the merlin, the kestrel, the sparrow-hawk, and the
buzzard. All these are considerably more abundant in
India than in the British Isles.

Thus far we have spoken chiefly of birds that are
found in the plains of India all the year round. We
have now to deal with migrants. As was to be
expected, many of these are common to Hindustan and
to England.

Surprising as it may seem, stationary birds are the
exception rather than the rule. The majority of
species, like viceroys and lieutenant-governors, divide
their time more or less equally between two different

places. It is by no means always easy to determine whether any particular species is a migrant one or not. The mere fact that specimens of it are seen in any given place at all seasons of the year is not sufficient to prove that it is non-migratory. For the birds of a species we saw six months ago are not necessarily the same ones that we have with us to-day. To take a concrete example, the crested lark (*Galerita cristata*) is found in Lahore all the year round, but is far more plentiful in summer than in winter, which is the only time when it is seen in England. The species is therefore a migratory one.

The general rule as regards migratory birds is that they breed in the north and then go south for a season to enjoy themselves. Great Britain is further north than India and has a much colder climate, hence we should expect birds to crowd to India for the pleasant cold weather and go to England for the genial summer. This does happen to a large extent. Yet there are surprisingly few birds which winter in India and summer in England. The only common ones that I can call to mind are the wagtails, the pipits, and the quail (*Coturnix communis*). There are two reasons for this. The first is that migration takes place in a more or less northerly and southerly direction, and the British Isles are not due north of India. The second reason is that England is a long way south of the Arctic Circle. Its winter is therefore not cold enough for the taste of many birds. Geese, ducks, and snipe are cold-loving creatures. Their idea of nice mild weather is the English winter ! In order to avoid anything in the shape of heat they migrate very far north in summer, and in winter, being driven southwards by the intense Arctic cold, spread themselves all over the temperate zone.   Thus it comes to pass that the full and the jack snipe, the grey lag-goose, the mallard, the gadwall, the pintail and the shoveller ducks, the widgeon and the teal, are winter visitors both to India and the British Isles. But whereas snipe, geese, and most ducks leave India for the hot weather, many of them remain in Great Britain for the summer and nest there.   It is probable that the birds which spend the winter in Great Britain go further north to breed, their place in the British Isles being taken by species that have wintered in Africa. The north of Scotland, even, is too far south to serve as a breeding place for some species.   The little jack snipe (*Gallinago gallinula*) is one of these ; he never breeds in England, whereas the common or full snipe (*Gallinago cœlestis*) does.   Hence the former is set down as a migrant in England, while the latter is thought to be a permanent resident.   In point of fact both are migrants, as we see in India, but while some full snipe find a Scotch summer cool enough for them to breed in, all jack snipe find it insufferably hot.

A curious fact regarding snipe in India is that these birds appear in the south earlier than they do in the north.   I do not know the earliest date after the end of the hot weather on which a snipe has been shot in the Punjab, but believe it to be considerably later than the last week in August, at which time snipe are regularly shot in the Madras Presidency.   This is not what we should have expected.   It is but reasonable to suppose that

THE REDSHANK. (TOTANUS CALIDRIS)
(One of the British birds found in India)

the earliest birds to arrive in India would take up their winter quarters in the north, and that the later arrivals, finding all eligible residences in the north already occupied, would go farther afield. The only explanation of the phenomenon which occurs to me is that the most northerly birds are the first to feel the approaching Arctic winter and so are the first to migrate. These, when they arrive in India, find the northern portion of the peninsula too hot for them, so pass on southwards until they come to the places where the temperature is at that season lower.

This article has already reached an undue length, yet quite a number of birds, more or less common in England and in India, have not been mentioned. On this account I owe apologies to the cuckoo, the stint, the sandpiper, the redshank, the ringed and the Kentish plovers. But the names of these and of eight score others, are they not written in the appendix?

THE BIRD IN BLUE

AS I write my tympanic membranes are being somewhat rudely shaken by the clamorous voices of a brood of young blue jays, which are in a nest somewhere in one of the chimneys of my bungalow.

From the point of view of the blue jays the site they have chosen for their nursery is an admirable one; indeed, had the architect of the bungalow received a handsome "tip" he could not have provided the birds with more comfortable accommodation.

The shaft of the chimney is not straight, as, in my humble opinion, it should be. At a few feet from the top it is bent at a right angle, and runs horizontally for a short distance before it again assumes what I consider to be its normal course.

The architect was, however, not such a fool as he may appear, for it is quite impossible to clean properly the chimney of his design; it must therefore take fire sooner or later, and the fire may spread and result in the destruction of the house. The re-erection thereof would of course mean more work for the said architect.

The blue jays are as satisfied as the designer with the chimney, because the horizontal portion forms a shelf

upon which they can lay their eggs. These are visible
neither from above nor from below, and they are as
inaccessible as invisible, for the chimney is so narrow as
to baffle all attempts at ascent or descent on the part
of human beings.

The blue jays make good to my ear what they deny
my eye. The young hopefuls utter unceasingly a loud
cry resembling that of some creature in distress. This
is what I have to listen to all the time I am in the
bungalow. Outside, the parent birds make the welkin
ring with their raucous voices. Never were father and
mother prouder of their offspring or fonder of pro-
claiming the fact. When not cumbered about much
serving they squat either on the roof or on a blue gum
tree hard by, and, at regular intervals, utter a short,
sharp, harsh " Tshow." This is emphasised by a jerk of
the tail ; the blue jay does nothing without first consult-
ing its caudal appendage.

On the occasions when I made vain attempts to
obtain a look at the young birds the parents took to
their wings, and, as they sped through the air, uttered
cries so harsh and dry-sounding as to make me feel
quite thirsty!

The blue jay is so familiar to us Anglo-Indians as to
need no description. We have all admired the bird as
it lazily sailed through the air on outstretched pinions
of pale blue and rich ultramarine. We have, each of us,
watched it perched on a railing looking out for its insect
quarry. It is then comparatively inconspicuous, its
neck and wing coverts being the hue of a faded port-
wine stain. We have seen it pounce upon some object

too small for us to distinguish, and either devour it then and there or bear it off in triumph.

We all know that the bird is not a jay at all, that its proper name is the Indian roller (*Coracias indica*), that it is related to the kingfisher family, and that it is called a jay merely on account of its gaudy plumage.

Next to its colour the most striking thing about the blue jay is its wonderful power of flight. Ordinarily the bird is content to flap along at an easy pace, but, when it likes, it can move for a little as though it were shot out of a catapult ; moreover, it is able to completely change its course with startling rapidity ; hence even the swiftest birds of prey find it no child's play to catch a roller bird. A good idea of its aerial performances may be obtained by watching it attack a kite that persists in hovering about in the neighbourhood of the nest. Blue jays, like king-crows and doves, are exceedingly short-tempered when they have young.

This species seems to indulge in very little sleep ; it is up betimes, and may be seen about long after every other day bird, with the possible exception of the king-crow, is fast asleep.

The blue jay is a good friend to the gardener, since it feeds exclusively on insects and small animals. Jerdon cites as the chief articles of its diet, large insects, grass-hoppers, crickets, mantidæ, and beetles, with an occa-sional field-mouse or shrew. To this list he might have added frogs and small snakes.

At most seasons of the year the blue jay strikes one as a rather sluggish bird, being content to squat on a perch for a great part of the day and wait patiently for

THE INDIAN ROLLER, OR "BLUE JAY." (CORACIAS INDICA)

quarry to come its way.   At the breeding season, however, it becomes very sprightly.   It is then more than
usually vociferous and indulges in a course of aerial
gymnastics.   It may be seen at these throughout the
month of March, now towering high above the earth,
then dropping headlong down, to suddenly check itself
and sail away, emitting the while the hoarsest and
wheeziest notes imaginable, and behaving generally
like the proverbial March hare.   These performances
are either actual love-making or a prelude to it.   By
the end of March the various birds have sorted themselves out, and then the billing and cooing stage begins.

At this season the birds are invariably found in
pairs ; the cock and hen delight to sit side by side on
some exposed branch.   Like the young couples that
moon about Hyde Park on Sundays, blue jays do not
mind spooning in public.   As the sexes dress alike
it is not possible to say which of a couple is the
cock and which is the hen.   Under such circumstances
naturalists always assume that the bird which makes
the advances is the cock.   I am not at all sure that
this assumption is justified.   Among human beings the
ladies very frequently set their caps at the men.   Why
should not the fair sex among birds do likewise?

In many species the sexes dress differently, and it is
then easy to discover which sex "makes the running,"
and in such cases this is by no means always the cock.
I have seen one hen paradise flycatcher drive away
another and then go and make up to a cock bird.   Similarly I have seen two hen orioles behave in a very un-
ladylike manner to one another, all because they both had

designs on the same cock. He sat and looked on from a distance at the contest, and would assuredly have purred with delight had he known how to do so! But of this more anon. The blue-jay lovers sit on a branch, side by side, and gaze upon one another with enraptured eyes. Suddenly one of them betakes itself to some other tree, uttering its hoarse screeches as it flies. Its companion follows almost immediately and then begins to bow and scrape, puff out its neck, slowly wave its tail, and utter unmusical cries. The bird which is being thus courted adds its voice to that of its companion. The raucous duet over, silence reigns for a little. Then one of the birds moves on, to be followed by its companion, and the above performance is repeated, and will continue to be repeated dozens of times before the birds give themselves over to family cares.

The greatest admirer of the blue jay could not call its nest a work of art. The eggs are laid in a hole in a tree or building. Usually the hole is more or less lined by a promiscuous collection of grass, tow, feathers, and the like, but sometimes the birds are content to lay their eggs in the bare cavity.

The blue jay, although so brazen over its courtship, strongly objects to having its family affairs pried into, so if you would find its nursery you must, unless you are lucky, exercise some patience. The birds steadfastly refuse to visit the nest when they know they are being watched. If patience be a virtue great, the blue jay is a most virtuous bird, for, if it is aware that it is being observed, it will take up a perch and sit there for hours, mournfully croaking, rather than betray the whereabouts of its eggs or young. Most of the nests I have seen have been discovered by accident. For example, when going along a road I have had occasion to look round suddenly at some bird flying overhead and caught sight of a roller entering a hole in a tree.

Some days ago I was out with a friend, when we saw a hoopoe, with food in its mouth, disappear into a hole in the wall of a Hindu temple. The aperture was about seven feet from the ground, so, in order to look into it, I mounted my friend's back. While I was investigating the hoopoe's hole, a blue jay flew out of another hole in the wall within a yard of my face!

Like Moses of old, I turned aside to investigate this new wonder, and found that the hole went two and a half feet into the wall, and that its aperture was a square six inches in both length and breadth. The floor of this little alcove was covered with earth and tiny bits of dirty straw, which may or may not have been put there by the blue jay. On this lay a clutch of four glossy white eggs, nearly as large as those laid by the degenerate Indian *murghi*. Fortunately for those blue jays I am not an egg collector. As it was, I did remove one of them for a lady who was anxious to have it, but this was not missed. Birds cannot count.

SPARROWS IN THE NURSERY

THE sparrow, as every Anglo-Indian knows, is a bird that goes about dumping down nests in *sahibs'* bungalows. It is greatly assisted in this noble work by the native of India, who has brought to the acme of perfection the art of jerry-building. In the ramshackle, half-finished modern bungalow the rafters that support the ceiling never, by any chance, fit properly into the walls. There are thus in every room a number of cracks, holes, and crevices in which the sparrows love to nest. As a matter of fact, these are not at all safe nesting places. Apart from the fact that the nest is liable to be pulled down at any moment by an angry human being, the situation is dangerous, because there is nothing to prevent a restless young bird from falling out of the nest and thus terminating a promising career. A few days ago a servant brought me a baby sparrow that had fallen out of a nest in the pantry. I always feel inclined to wring the neck of any sparrow that fate has put within my grasp, for I have many a score to pay off against the species. Upon this occasion, however, I felt mercifully inclined, so took the young bird, which was nearly covered with feathers, and offered it bread soaked in milk. This it swallowed greedily. When the youngster was as full up inside as the Hammersmith 'bus on a wet day, I told the bearer to put it in the cage in which my amadavats dwell. When I left for office I directed the man to feed the new arrival. On my return in the evening the bearer informed me that the young hopeful had declined its food. Now, a young sparrow refuses to eat only when it is stuffed to the brim. It was thus evident that its parents had found it out and were feeding it, in spite of the fact that the nest from which it came was in the pantry on the east side of the house, while its new quarters were in the west verandah.

The next day a second sparrow fell out of the nest in the pantry and was also consigned to the amadavats' cage. At bed-time that night I took a look at the birds, and found that the two young sparrows had tucked themselves snugly in the seed tin! The next morning a third sparrow from the same nest was brought to me; it was put in the cage along with its brethren. As my office was closed on the day in question, I had the cage placed in front of my study window. I could thus watch the doings of the latest additions to my aviary. The hen sparrow does the lion's share of the feeding; she works like a slave from morning to night. At intervals, varying from one to ten minutes, throughout the day she appears with a beakful of food, which consists chiefly of green caterpillars.

It is the custom to speak of the sparrow as a curse to the husbandman. The bird is popularly supposed to live on grain, fruit, seedlings, and buds—those of

c

valuable plants by preference.   There is no denying
the fact that the sparrow does devour a certain amount
of fruit and grain, but, so far from being a pest, I
believe that the good it does by destroying noxious
insects far outweighs the harm.   Adult sparrows frequently feed on insects.   I have watched them hawking
flies in company with the swifts, and the skill displayed
by the "spadger" showed that his was no 'prentice
hand at the game.

Sparrow nestlings in the early stages are fed almost
exclusively on caterpillars, grubs, and insects.   As there
are usually five or six baby sparrows in a brood, and as
these have appalling appetites, they must consume an
enormous number of insects.   Let us work out a little
sum.   We may assume that the sparrow brings at
least three caterpillars in each beakful of food she
carries to her brood.   She feeds them at least fifteen
times in the hour, and works for not less than twelve
hours in the day.   I timed the sparrows in question to
commence feeding operations at 5.30 a.m., and when I
left the bungalow at 6 p.m. the birds were still at it.
Thus the hen sparrow brings in something like 540
insects *per diem* to her brood.   She feeds them on this
diet for at least twenty days, so that the brood is responsible for no less than 10,000 insects, mostly caterpillars, before its units are ready to fend for themselves.
According to Hume, the sparrow in India brings up
two broods in the year.   I should have doubled this
figure, since the species appears to be always breeding.
But it is better to understate than exaggerate.   We
thus arrive at the conclusion that the hen sparrow

destroys each year over 20,000 insects, mostly injurious, in the feeding of her young. Add to this number those she herself consumes, those the cock eats, and those he brings to the nest, and you have a fine insect mortality bill.

The movements of the mother bird when feeding her young are so rapid that it is not easy to determine what it is she brings to the nest, even though the objects hang down from her beak ; the same applies to the cock. In order to make quite certain of the nature of the food she was bringing, I sought, by frightening her, to make her drop a beakful ; accordingly, at one of her visits I tapped the window-pane smartly just as she was about to ram the food down the gaping mouth of a young bird. She flew off chirruping with anger and alarm, but kept her bill tightly closed on the food she was carrying. As the parents had to feed the young ones through the bars of a cage the process required some manipulation, and, in spite of its care, the bird sometimes dropped part of its burden ; but, almost before I had time to move, it had dashed down to the ground and retrieved it. However, by dint of careful watching I managed to bang the window immediately after the hen had dropped something of a dark colour. Having frightened her away I rushed outside and found that the object in question was part of a sausage-shaped sac containing a number of tiny green grubs. After a few minutes the hen returned with her beak full. Her fright had made her suspicious, so she perched on the verandah trellis-work and looked around for a little. Nine times she flew towards the cage, but on each occasion her courage failed her, to the intense disgust of her clamouring brood. At the tenth attempt she plucked up sufficient courage to feed the young birds.

At a subsequent visit she dropped a caterpillar, and I frightened her away before she could retrieve it. I found it to be alive and about an inch in length.

On another occasion I saw her ramming something black down the throat of a young hopeful. Frightening her away, I went outside and found the youthful bird making valiant attempts to swallow a whole mulberry. But it was not often that she gave them fruit; green caterpillars formed quite nine-tenths of what she brought in; the remainder was composed chiefly of grubs, with an occasional grasshopper or moth. As the young grew older the proportion of insect food given to them diminished until, when they were about twenty-two days old, their diet was made up principally of grain.

The day on which the third young sparrow was put into the cage was a warm one, so at 2 p.m., when the shade temperature was about 115°, I brought the cage into the comparatively cool bungalow, for the sake of the amadavats. The cock sparrow witnessed the removal of the cage and did not hesitate to give me a bit of his mind. In a minute or so the hen returned with her beak full of green caterpillars. When she found the cage gone, she, too, expressed her opinion of me and of mankind in general in no uncertain terms. It was the last straw. Earlier in the day I had removed one of the baby sparrows from the cage and placed it in a cigar-ash tray outside the cage. The hen had affected not to notice that anything had happened, and fed it in the ash-tray as though she were unconscious of the removal. When, however, the whole cage and its contents disappeared it was quite useless for her to pretend that nothing was wrong, so she treated me to her best " Billingsgate."

After the cage had been inside for about three-quarters of an hour the young "spadgers" began to feel the pangs of hunger, and made this known by giving vent to a torrent of chirrups which differed in no way from those that make the adult so offensive. All that the poor mother could do was to answer from the outside. I felt, that afternoon, that I was paying off with interest some of my score against the sparrow.

The next day I did not take the cage into the bunga-low, because I wanted to ascertain whether sparrows feed their young throughout the day, or whether they indulge in a noonday siesta. They kept it up, at their respective rates, throughout the day, although the ther-mometer in the shade must have risen to 115°. After the hen had disburdened herself of the food she brought, she would perch for a moment on the trellis, and pant with open beak as though she were thoroughly ex-hausted.

I have long been trying to ascertain how birds in the nest obtain the liquid they require. Do the succulent caterpillars, on which young sparrows are fed, provide them with sufficient moisture, or do the parents water them? Although I spent several hours in watching those sparrows, I am not able to answer the question satisfactorily. I placed a bowl of water on the ground near the cage, hoping that this would tempt the hen bird to drink, and that I should see her carry some of the liquid to her offspring. But she took no notice of the water. She certainly used to come to the cage sometimes with her beak apparently empty, and yet insert it into the open mouth of a young one. Was she then watering the nestling, or did her beak hold some small seeds that did not protrude? It seems incredible that unfledged birds exposed to the temperature of an Indian summer require no water; nevertheless, I never actually saw any pass from the crop of the parents to those of the youngsters.

THE CARE OF YOUNG BIRDS
AFTER THEY LEAVE THE NEST

IT has been urged as an objection to the Darwinian theory that Natural Selection, if that force exists, must tend to destroy species rather than cause new ones to come into being. Nearly all birds leave the nest before they are fully developed. When they first come out of the nursery they have attained neither their full powers of flight nor complete skill in obtaining food. Every young bird, no matter how fine a specimen it be, leaves the nest an inexperienced weakling, and can therefore stand no chance in competition with the fully grown and experienced members of the species. Natural Selection takes an individual as it finds it and pays no attention to potentialities.

That such an objection should have been urged against the theory of Natural Selection is proof of the fact that naturalists are inclined to forget that, with many, if not all, species of birds, the duties of the parents towards their offspring by no means cease when the young birds leave the nest.

The parent birds, in many cases, continue to feed their young long after these are apparently well able to fend for themselves. This fact is not sufficiently emphasised in books on natural history. On the other hand, such works lay stress upon the fact that in many species of birds the parents drive their offspring away from the place of their birth in order that the numbers of the species in the locality shall not outgrow the food supply. How far this is a general characteristic of birds I do not know. What I desire to emphasise is that the driving-away process, when it occurs, does not take place until some time after the young have left the nest. The fact that the parent birds tend the young long after they have left the nest, and even after they are fully capable of holding their own in the struggle for existence, disposes of the above-cited objection to the theory of Natural Selection. Nature is so careful of the young warriors that she prolongs the instinct of parental affection longer than is absolutely necessary. So important is it that the young should have a fair start in life that she errs on the safe side.

It is common knowledge that foster-parents feed cuckoos when these have grown so large that, in order to reach the mouth of their spurious babes, the little foster-mothers have to perch on their shoulders.

The sight of a tiny bird feeding the great parasite is laughable, but it is also most instructive. It demonstrates how thoroughly bird mothers perform their duties.

Crows tend their young ones for weeks after they have left the nest. I have had ample opportunity of satisfying myself as to this.

It was my custom in Madras to breakfast on the verandah. A number of crows used to assemble daily to watch operations and to pick up the pieces of food

thrown to them.   They would go farther when the
opportunity occurred, and commit petty larceny.

The crows were all grey-necked ones, with the exception of two belonging to the larger black species.   But
these latter are comparatively shy birds, and consequently used to hang about on the outskirts of the
crowd.

Among the grey-necked crows was a family of four
—the parents and two young birds.   Every day, without
fail, they used to visit the verandah ; the two young
birds made more noise than all the rest of the crows
put together.   They were easily recognisable, firstly, by
their more raucous voices, and, secondly, by the pink
inside of the mouth.   When I first noticed them they
were so old that, in size, they were very nearly equal to
the mother.   Further, the grey of the neck was sharply
differentiated from the black portions of the plumage,
showing that they had left the nest some time ago.

Unfortunately I did not make a note of the day
on which they first put in an appearance.   I can,
however, safely say that they visited my verandah
regularly for some weeks, during the whole of which
time the mother bird fed them most assiduously.   It was
ludicrous to see the great creatures sidle up to mamma
when she had seized a piece of toast, and open their
red mouths, often pecking at one another out of
jealousy.

They were obviously well able to look after themselves; their flight was as powerful as that of the mother
bird, yet she treated them as though they were infants,
incapable of doing anything for themselves.

At the beginning of the cold weather I changed my quarters, so was not able to witness the break-up of the crow family. Probably this did not occur until the following spring, when nesting operations commenced.

The feeding of the young after they have left the nest and are full-grown is not confined to crows.

I was walking one morning along a shady lane when I noticed on the grass by the roadside a bird which I did not recognise. It was a small creature, clothed in black and white, which tripped along like a wagtail. It had no tail, but it wagged the hind end of its body just as a sandpiper does. While I was trying to identify this strange creature, a young pied wagtail came running up to it with open mouth, into which the first bird popped something. I then saw that the unknown bird was simply a pied wagtail (*Motacilla maderaspatensis*) which had lost her tail! The young bird was fully as large as the mother, and having a respectable tail, which it wagged in a very sedate manner, looked far more imposing. The parts of the plumage which were black in the mother were brownish grey in the young bird. The white eyebrow was not so well defined in the youngster as in the adult, while the former had rather more white in the wing, but as regards size there was nothing to choose between the two. The young bird remained in close attendance on the mother. It was able to keep pace with her as she dashed after a flying insect. It ran after her begging continually for food. The mother swallowed most of the flies she caught, but now and again put one into the mouth of the young bird, but she did so very severely, as if she were saying, "You are far too old to be fed ; it is no use to pretend you cannot catch insects, you are a naughty, lazy, little bird!" But the lackadaisical air of the young one expressed more plainly than words : "Oh, mother, it tires me to chase insects. They move so fast. I have tried, but have caught so few, and am very hungry."

For several minutes the young wagtail followed the mother ; then something arrested its attention, so that it tarried behind its parent. The mother moved away, apparently glad to be rid of the troublesome child for a little. Then she suddenly flew off. Presently the young wagtail looked round for its mother, and I was interested to see what would happen when it noticed that she had flown away. My curiosity was soon satisfied. Directly the young bird perceived that the mother had gone, it set itself most philosophically to catch insects, which it did with all the skill of an old bird, turning, twisting, doubling, with the elegance of an experienced wagtail.

I describe these two little incidents, not as anything wonderful, but as examples of what is continually going on in the world around us.

The parental instinct is probably developed in some birds more than in others, but I believe that in all cases the affection of a bird mother for her young persists long after they have left the nest, and for some time after they are fully capable of looking after themselves.

Birds are born with many instincts, but they have much to learn both before and after they leave the nest.

It is not until their education is complete, until the mother bird has taught them all she herself knows, until they are as strong or stronger than she, that the young birds are driven away and made to look after themselves.

THE INDIAN ADJUTANT. (LEPTOPTILUS DUBIUS)

THE ADJUTANT BIRD

THE adjutant bird (*Leptoptilus dubius*) is one of Nature's little jokes. It is a caricature of a bird, a mixture of gravity and clownishness. Everything about it is calculated to excite mirth—its weird figure, its great beak, its long, thin legs, its conspicuous pouch, its bald head, and every attitude it strikes. The adjutant bird is a stork which has acquired the habits of the vulture. Forsaking to a large extent frogs and such-like delicacies, which constitute the normal diet of its kind, it lives chiefly upon offal. Now, most, if not all, birds which feed on carrion have the head and neck devoid of feathers. This arrangement, if not ornamental, is very useful. The bare head and neck are, as "Eha" remarks, "the sleeves tucked up for earnest work." The adjutant forms no exception to the rule, it wears the badge of its profession. But let me here give a full description of this truly comic bird. It stands five feet in its stockings. Its bill is over a foot in length and correspondingly massive. As we have seen, the whole head and neck are bare, except for a few feathers scattered over it like the hairs on an elephant's head. The bare skin is not lacking in colour. On the forehead it is blackish; it becomes saffron-yellow on the upper neck, while lower down it turns to brick-red. There is a ruff of white feathers round the base of the neck. This ruff, of course, appears entirely out of place and adds to the general grotesqueness of the bird. The back and wings are ashy black, becoming slaty grey at the breeding season. The lower parts are white.

As if the creature, thus arrayed, were not sufficiently comic, Nature has given it a great pouch which dangles from the neck. This is over a foot in length and hangs down like a bag when inflated. It is red in colour, spotted with black. Its situation naturally leads one to believe that it is connected with the gullet, that it is a receptacle into which the bird can hastily pass the garbage it swallows pending more complete disposal. But it is nothing of the sort. It does not communicate directly with the œsophagus. Knowing this, one is able to appreciate to the full the splendid mendacity of the writer to *Chambers's Journal* in 1861, who declares that he witnessed an adjutant swallow a crow which he watched " pass into the sienna-toned pouch of the gaunt avenger. He who writes saw it done."

Note the last sentence. The scribe was evidently of opinion that people would not believe him, so thought to clinch matters by bluffing! But, to do him justice, it is quite possible that he did see an adjutant swallow a crow, for other observers have witnessed this, but the remainder of the story rests upon the sandy foundation of the imagination. If the truth must be told, we do not know for certain what the use of this pouch is. Blyth suggested that it is analogous to the air cell attached to one lung only of the python or the boa-constrictor, and, as in that case, no doubt supplies oxygen to the lungs during protracted meals. The bird can thus "guzzle" to its heart's content without having to stop every now and then to take a "breather."

But we must return to the appearance of the bird, for the account of this is not yet complete, since no mention has been made of the eye. This is white and very small, and so gives the bird a wicked, knowing expression, like that of an elephant. Colonel Cunningham speaks of "the malignantly sneaking expression of the pallid eyes." This is perhaps a little severe on the adjutant, but it is, I fear, quite useless to deny the fact that he has "a canister look in his heye."

A mere description of the shape and colouring of the adjutant does not give any idea of his comicality. It is his acts rather than his appearance that make him so ludicrous. Except when floating high above the earth on his great pinions the bird always looks grotesque. To say that he, as he walks along, recalls a hunch-backed old man who is deliberately "clowning" is to give a hopelessly inadequate idea of the absurdity of his movements. Lockwood Kipling is nearer the mark when he says: "For grotesque devilry of dancing the Indian adjutant beats creation. Don Quixote or Malvolio were not half so solemn or mincing, and yet there is an abandonment and lightness of step, a wild lift in each solemn prance, which are almost demoniacal. If it were possible for the most angular, tall, and demure of elderly maiden ladies to take a great deal too much champagne and then to give a lesson in ballet dancing, with occasional pauses of acute sobriety, perhaps some faint idea might be conveyed of the peculiar quality of the adjutant's movements."

Sometimes the bird struts along solemnly with bent back and forwardly pointed bill, at others it will jump or skip along with outstretched wings and clap its beak. It cannot even stand still without striking ludicrous attitudes. Seen from behind, it looks like a little hunch-backed old man with very thin legs, dressed in a grey swallow - tail coat. Adjutants sometimes vary the monotony of existence by standing on one leg; occasionally they sit down, stretching their long legs out in front, and looking " as though they were kneeling wrong side foremost."

Colonel Cunningham gives a most entertaining account of the habits of these birds, many of which used, until quite recently, to be seen about Calcutta. My observations are chiefly confined to birds in captivity; this perhaps accounts for the fact that they do not agree in all respects with those of the Colonel. According to him, adjutants "are singularly ill-tempered birds, constantly squabbling with one another, even in the absence of any cause of competition, such as favourite roosts or specially savoury stores of offal. Even whilst several of them are standing quietly about, sunning themselves and apparently buried in deep thought, a quarrel will suddenly arise for no apparent reason ; and then you may see two monstrous fowls begin to pace around, cautiously stalking one another, and watching for a favourable opportunity of striking and buffeting with beak and wings. The expression of slow malignity with which such duellists regard one another is gruesome, and the injuries resulting from the fray are often ghastly; blinded eyes and bloody cocks-combs being matters of everyday occurrence."

Captive adjutants seem to be most placid birds. There are three of them in the "Zoo" at Lahore, kept in a large park-like enclosure, and I have never seen these fighting. They appear to be always, if not on the best of terms, at any rate, indifferent to one another. The three will stand for many minutes at a time in a row, motionless as statues. Sometimes a male and a female will huddle up to one another and remain thus, with their heads almost touching, looking like carica-tures of Darby and Joan.

The table manners of adjutants, like those of most other carrion feeders, are not polite. I will therefore not attempt to describe them. In the good old days, feeding adjutants used to be a favourite pastime of Mr. Thomas Atkins at Calcutta. I regret to have to say that his motives were not always purely philan-thropic. To connect two pieces of meat by a long string and then throw them among a crowd of adju-tants savours of practical joking. One bird, of course, swallows one piece of meat, while a second adjutant secures the other morsel. All goes well until each of the birds tries to go its own way—then a tug-of-war results, fraught with gastronomical disturbance to the combatants.

Adjutants are nowhere very abundant; they are nevertheless spread over the whole of Northern India, but do not appear to be found so far south as Madras. Another species, however—the smaller adju-

D

tant (*L. javanicus*)—has been observed on the Malabar coast.

Some natives make adjutant-catching their profession. The birds are captured on account of their down-like feathers, which are of considerable commercial value.

The catcher fits the skin of an adjutant over his head and shoulders, and in this attire creeps up to a company of the birds as they stand half-asleep, knee-deep in water. Great is the surprise of the unsuspecting birds when one of them is unceremoniously seized by the wolf in the adjutant's skin.

THE INDIAN ADJUTANT. (LEPTOPTILUS DUBIUS)

THE SARUS

HAVING discoursed upon the adjutant, it seems but fitting that we should turn our attention to another long-shanked gentleman—the sarus. The adjutant is, as we have seen, a stork, while the sarus is a crane. I do not know whether this conveys very much information to the average mind. Most people will, I imagine, "give it up" if asked, "What is the difference between a stork and a crane?" Yet there are considerable differences between the two; they belong to different families, and, like rival tradesmen of the same name, "have no connection with one another." I do not propose to detail the anatomical differences between storks and cranes, for the excellent reason that I myself do not know them all, nor have I the least intention of acquiring such knowledge. It forms part of the dry bones of science, and these are best left to museum ornithologists to squabble over. There are, however, one or two simple points which suffice to enable us to distinguish at a glance a crane from a stork. The hind toe of the stork is well developed, while that of the crane is small and does not touch the ground; the consequence is that the stork likes to rest on trees, while the crane prefers to stand on *terra firma* on its flat feet.

The nostrils of the crane are half-way down the beak, while they are at the base in the bill of the stork. The crane nests on the ground; the stork builds in a tree. Young storks are helpless creatures, while little cranes hop and run about from the moment they leave the egg. Lastly, the crane has a voice, a fine loud voice, a voice that can be heard a mile away, a voice like a trumpet, for its windpipe is coiled. King stork, on the other hand, has no voice; when he wants to make a joyful noise he is obliged to clap together his great mandibles.

Cranes have been favourites with man from time immemorial. The result is that ancient and mediæval writers have plenty to say about them. Now the naturalist of old considered himself in honour bound to attribute some wonderful characteristic to every beast of which he wrote. If he did not know of any clever thing done by any creature, he invented something for it to do. This method had the advantage of making natural history a very exciting and interesting study. Cranes were supposed to perform all manner of tricks with stones. As we have seen, they are blessed with powerful voices, and, like other loud-voiced people, find it difficult to keep silent. They are fully persuaded that silence is golden; but, when it comes to acting up to this belief, the flesh proves itself very frail. Thus it came to pass that the sagacious birds, when migrating, used to stop up their mouths with stones. As they are far too well-bred to speak with the mouth full, they were able to maintain a decorous silence when travelling.

I can cite plenty of authority for this statement. There is, in particular, no less a personage than "Robert Tanner, Gent. Practitioner in Astrologie and Physic." "The cranes," he writes, "when they fly out of Cilicia, over the mountain Taurus, carried in their mouths a pebble stone, lest by their chattering they should be ceased upon by eagles."

The cranes had yet another use for their stones. When the main body were resting at night, sentinels were posted to guard against surprise, so that the company could go to sleep in security. To ensure necessary vigilance, the sentinels stood on one foot and held in the other a large stone. If they inadvertently nodded, their muscles relaxed and the stone dropped. This, of course, used to wake them up. Even Alexander the Great was glad to learn a lesson from the cranes. He used to go to roost with, not a stone in his hands, but a silver ball, as more befitting his royal dignity. On the slightest movement the ball would fall and he wake up. Thus it was that he never overslept himself. We do not do such heroic things nowadays ; nor do cranes.

Cranes are birds which will not stand nonsense. The pigmies used to go egg-collecting among them ; the result of this was, to translate Homer :—

> When inclement winters vex the plain,
> With piercing frosts, or thick descending rain,
> To warmer seas the cranes embodied fly,
> With noise and order, through the midway sky :
> To pigmy nations wound and death they bring.

Notice that as the cranes were on the war-path there was no necessity for them to fill their mouths with stones ; they wanted all their lung power to bark at their pigmy foes.

Having considered cranes as they are not, it behoves us to glance at them as they are. The sarus is a handsome creature. It stands over five feet high. The general colour of the plumage is a beautiful French grey. The head and long neck are devoid of feathers, but are covered with numerous tiny crimson warts or papillæ. These assume a deeper hue at the breeding season, which occurs from July to September. There is a patch of grey on the sides of the head. The throat and a ring round the nape are covered with black hairs.

Saruses feed upon vegetable substances, insects, earthworms, frogs, lizards, and other small reptiles, with an occasional snake thrown in by way of condiment. "This," remarks Babu Ram Brama Sanyal, "shows the kind of accommodation they must have."

Saruses are not gregarious birds, but hunt in couples and are said to mate for life. It is further asserted that when one of a pair is killed the other pines away and dies. I believe this to be true, although I cannot vouch for it, and am certainly not going to put the statement to the test by shooting one of a pair : for these cranes are such tame, confiding birds that to shoot them savours strongly of murder.

According to Jerdon, a young sarus is not bad eating, but old birds are worthless for the table. Lucky old birds! Saruses thrive very well in captivity. As they habitually indulge in all manner of eccentric dances they make most amusing pets. They are usually gentle and let strangers caress them and tickle their heads. But I always let others try this on for the first time with a strange crane, because some birds resent this head-tickling and, to again quote from the worthy Babu above mentioned, "appear to exist only as it were for pecking at everything, bird, beast, and man: children being the special object of their wrath."

There are two cranes in the "Zoo" at Lahore; they are a most mischievous couple. They used to be kept with the ducks and geese, and amused themselves by rooting up all freshly planted rushes. At feeding time it was their habit to hop from one dish of food to another with outstretched wings and thus frighten off the ducks and secure the lion's share for themselves. They were then removed to the enclosure where the adjutants are. They started playing tricks on these, but the adjutant has a powerful beak which he is quite ready to use when necessity arises. The result is that the saruses are not on speaking terms with the adjutants.

Unlike the adjutant, whose nest is a huge platform of sticks placed on the top of a very lofty tree, the sarus builds its nursery on the ground. This takes the form of a large cone, several feet in diameter at the base and two or three feet high. It is composed of reeds, rushes, and straw, and placed by preference in shallow water. Great care is taken to keep the eggs above water level. If, as is apt to happen in India, heavy rain comes on after the completion of the nest, the parents speedily set to work to raise the eggs by adding more material to that upon which they rest.

THE STABILITY OF SPECIES

IF two crows be taken to an ornithologist and he be told that one of them was caught in the Himalayas while the other was captured in Madras, he will not be able to tell which individual came from which area: in other words, the crows of Madras resemble those of the Himalayas. This, of course, is no unusual phenomenon. The same may be said of the myna, the king-crow, and a great many other birds and beasts. Yet the phenomenon is a remarkable one if we take into account the facts of variation.

If several hundred thousand crows be collected and carefully examined, it will be found that no two of them resemble one another in all respects. This being so, we should expect the crows of Madras to differ from those of the Himalayas, since the two environments are so dissimilar. We may say with tolerable certainty that no intercrossing takes place between the crows of the two localities: for these birds are stay-at-home creatures, and do not wander far afield. In this case, therefore, it is not intercrossing that has prevented the origin of local races.

A consideration of the main causes which conduce to the stability of species may not be devoid of in-

terest ; for the subject is one which has hitherto attracted but little attention.   Since the Darwinian
hypothesis was given to the world we have heard so
much of variation and the origin of new species that
the other phenomenon—that of the fixity of species—in
spite of varying environments has been almost entirely
overlooked.   Yet it was just this feature of animal life
that attracted the attention of the older zoologists and
led them to believe that species had been created once
and for all, and that, when created, they were immutably
fixed.

Most biologists, if asked to explain the comparative
fixity of species, the slowness of evolution, would, I
think, refer to the fact that variations appear to take
place indiscriminately in all directions.   Take, for
example, a large number of birds of any species and
measure any one organ, let us say the first primary
wing feather. Suppose the average length be six inches.
We shall find that in a considerable percentage of the
individuals measured the wing is exactly six inches in
length : that six inches is what we may call the favourite or fashionable length of the wing.   The next commonest lengths will be 5·99 and 6·01 inches, and so on.
We shall find that only a very small percentage of the
individuals have wings shorter than 5½ inches or longer
than 6½ inches ; and if we measured a thousand individuals we probably should not find any in which the
wing was shorter than five inches or longer than seven.

Now, the commonly accepted theory is that in those
cases where there is free interbreeding the long-winged
varieties and the short-winged varieties tend to neutralise

one another, hence no change in character takes place. The effects of variation are swamped by intercrossing. It is only when intercrossing is checked, as when natural selection weeds out certain varieties, that evolution occurs.

This theory, of course, explains, or helps to explain, why species are so stable; but it involves the assumption that there is no such thing as sexual selection among animals in a state of nature. The theory assumes that individuals mate in a haphazard manner, that a long-winged hen is as likely to select a short-winged husband as a long-winged one. Are we justified in assuming this? At present there is little evidence on the subject. Evidence can only be procured by measuring a number of pairs of birds that have mated, and seeing whether large hens mate chiefly with large cocks or with small cocks, or indifferently with large or small cock-birds.

That sexual selection is a reality and not a mere hypothesis there can, I think, be but little doubt. It is with the theory that supposes that the females alone exercise selection that I feel compelled to quarrel. The male selects his partner just as much as the female selects hers. The choice is mutual.

In the Zoological Gardens at Lahore there are a number of ordinary coloured peacocks and a number of albinos. No coloured hen will mate with a coloured cock if she is allowed to exercise a choice between him and an albino. Here, then, is a clear example of sexual selection.

Professor Karl Pearson has spent much time in trying

to discover whether there is such a thing as sexual selection—what we may call unconscious selection—among human beings. His experiments tend to show that there is.

If we take a thousand married men whose stature is not less than six feet, and a thousand also who are none of them taller than 5 ft. 8 in., we shall find that the average height of the wives of the former is greater than that of the wives of the shorter men.

If wild animals display a similar characteristic, it is evident that to say that intercrossing swamps variation and causes species to remain stable is not altogether accurate ; for, if like select like as partners, we should expect a number of races to rapidly arise, or, at any rate, three races—a large, medium, and small one. So far, however, as we can see, species display no such tendency. We are therefore driven to the conclusion either that there is among species in a state of nature no tendency for like individuals to select like as their partners, or, if there be such a tendency, there is some force at work which counteracts it.

It may be thought that the case of the peafowl in the Lahore "Zoo" tends to show that among animals it is dissimilarity, not similarity, that attracts, for the coloured hens mate with white cocks in preference to those like themselves.

As a matter of fact the hens select the white cocks, not because they are white, but because of the strength of the sexual instincts of these latter. The white cocks continually show off before the hens ; the sexual desire is developed more highly in them

than in the ordinary cocks, and it is this that attracts
the hens.

We must also bear in mind that abnormal variations
have a strong tendency to perpetuate themselves. If
a white cock mates with an ordinary peahen, the
majority of the offspring are pure white.

If there be such a thing as sexual selection, and
if it be, as I believe, the strongest, the most mettle-
some individuals, those in which the sexual instincts
reach the highest development, that attract the opposite
sex, then the question arises: is there any connection
between these characteristics and the size and colour
of their possessor ?   We are not in possession of
sufficient data to answer this question in the affirmative.
Nevertheless I believe that such a relation does exist.

The researches of Professor Pearson seem to point to
the fact that there exists a definite relation between
variation and fertility.   For every species there is a
mode or typical size and form, and from this there are
deviations in all directions, and, speaking generally, the
greater the deviation from the mode the less the fertility
of the individual.

If this be a general law we have here a very potent
factor tending to make species stable.   Those individuals which deviate least from the common type are
the most fertile ; they produce the most offspring ;
moreover, they are the most numerous, hence they, by
sheer force of numbers, keep a species stable.   The
abnormal individuals are comparatively few in number,
and they beget comparatively few of their kind, so have
no chance of establishing themselves and crushing out

the normal type, unless natural selection steps in to their aid.

Is comparative infertility the result of feebleness of the sexual instinct? If so, sexual selection must be conducive to the stability of species.

For if the rule be the greater the deviation of an individual from the normal the less the development in it of the sexual instinct and the less its fertility, it follows that an abnormal organism is less likely to find a mate than a normal individual is; and if it do succeed in forming a union, that union will probably produce less than the average number of offspring.

THE AMADAVAT

"GENTLEMEN," said a Cambridge professor to his class, "I regret that owing to the forgetfulness of my assistant, I am unable to show you a specimen of the shell of the mollusc of which we are speaking. You have, however, but to step into the parlour of any seaside lodging-house and on the mantelpiece you will see two of the shells in question." Every undergraduate immediately knew what the shell was like; so will my readers at once recognise the bird of which I write when I inform them that the amadavat is the little red bird with white spots that occurs in every aviary in India. The bird is, indeed, not all red, but the bill is bright red and there are patches of this colour all over the plumage—more in the cock than in the hen, and more in the former in the breeding season than at other times. Thus the general effect is that of a red bird; hence the native name *Lal munia*, which, being interpreted, is the red munia. This is the proper English name of the bird, although fanciers frequently call it the red waxbill. Men of science know it as *Sporæginthus amandava*. I may say here that the name avadavat or amadavat is derived from Ahmedabad, whence great numbers used to be exported, for the bird is a great favourite in England.

It is the cage bird of India *par excellence*. Hundreds of thousands of amadavats must at this moment be living in captivity. The bird takes to cage life as a Scotsman to whisky. Within five minutes of capture the little creature is contentedly eating its seed and singing quite gaily. This is no exaggeration. I was recently out with a friend when we came upon a small boy catching munias. We saw captured a fine cock which my friend purchased for two annas. Not happening to have a cage in his pocket, he put the tiny creature into a fold of his handkerchief and placed the remainder of the handkerchief in his pocket. While we were walking home our captive began twittering in answer to his companions who were still free. If this be not philosophical behaviour, I do not know what is.

Nothing is easier than to catch munias. All that is required is the common, pyramidal-shaped, four-anna wicker cage in which birds are usually carried about in India. To the base of one of the walls of this a flap is attached by a hinge. The flap is the same size and shape as the wall of the cage, and composed of a frame over which a narrow-meshed string net is stretched. A string is fastened to the apex of the flap. The cage, with a captive bird inside, is placed in the open so that the flap rests on the ground. On this some groundsel is thrown. In a few minutes a passing amadavat is attracted to the cage by the song of the bird inside. The new-comer at once begins to feed on the groundsel. Then the bird-catcher, who is seated a few yards away, pulls the string sharply, so that the flap closes over the side of the cage and thus the bird is secured. It is then placed inside the cage and the flap again set. In this manner a dozen or more amadavats can be captured in an hour.   As nine red munias are sold for a rupee, and as they will live for years in captivity and cost next to nothing to keep, it is not surprising that they are popular pets.

Moreover, the amadavat is no mean songster. "Eha" is, I think, a little severe on the bird when he states that "fifty in a cage make an admirable chorus." The bird is small, so is its voice, but what there is of the latter is exceedingly sweet. Were its notes only louder the bird would be in the first rank as a songster. A rippling stream of cheery twitters emanates unceasingly from a cage of munias. The birds seem never to tire. The cock frequently utters, in addition to this perpetual twitter, a warble of five or six notes. The birds love to huddle together in a row on a perch and twitter in chorus. Suddenly the chorus ceases ; one of the birds raises his head above the level of the others and sings a solo, while the rest listen in silence with the air of connoisseurs. When he has finished, another bird has a "turn," then another. The whole performance always puts me in mind of one of those impromptu concerts which soldiers are so fond of getting up.

Quite apart from their song, munias afford him who keeps them much pleasure, because they are most amusing birds to watch. They are very fond of heat. They are happiest when the thermometer stands at about a hundred. When they huddle together for the sake of warmth, all are content except the two end birds, who are kept warm only on one

side. No bird, therefore, likes to be an outside one
of a row. If two or three, sitting close together, are
joined by another, this last does not take up a position
at the end of the line. He knows a trick worth two of
that. He perches on the backs of two in the middle
and tries to wedge himself in between them. Sometimes he succeeds. Sometimes he does not. When he
does succeed he frequently upsets the equilibrium of
the whole row.

Needless to say, the birds roost huddled together, and
at bed-time there is great manœuvring to avoid an
outside position. Each tries to get somewhere in the
middle, and, in order to do so, adopts one of two
methods. He either flops on top of birds already in
position, and, if he cannot wedge himself in, sleeps
with one foot on the back of one bird and the other
on its neighbour's back. The birds do not seem to
mind being sat upon in this way. The other method
is for the two outer birds to press inwards until one of
those in the middle of the row is squeezed so hard
as to lose its foothold and be violently ejected upwards.
The bird thus jockeyed out of its position then hops to
one end and in its turn begins to push inwards, and so
the process continues until the birds grow too sleepy to
struggle any more. All this contest is conducted without a sound. There is no bickering or squabbling.
The only thing I know like it is the contest in the
dining-room of an Indian hotel, when two "boys,"
each belonging to a different master, seize a dish
simultaneously. Each is determined to secure that
dish, and neither dares utter a sound for fear of

E

angering his *Sahib*.   Thus they struggle in grim
silence.   Eventually one is victorious and walks off
in triumph with the dish.   The defeated servant at
once accepts the situation ; so is it with a munia ejected
from a central position.

Although amadavats are widely distributed in India
and fairly common in most parts of the country, they
usually escape notice on account of their small size.
When flying overhead they are probably mistaken for
sparrows.   Moreover, they do not often visit gardens ;
they prefer open country.

Amadavats belong to the finch family, to the great tribe
which includes the sparrow, the canary, and the weaver-
bird.   By their coarse, stout beak, tapering to a point,
you may know them.   The use of this big beak is to
husk grain.   Finches do not gobble up their seed whole
as pigeons or fowls do ; they carefully husk each grain
before swallowing it.   Hence the meal of a bird of this
family is a somewhat protracted affair.   He who keeps
an aviary should remember this and provide his birds
with several seed-boxes, otherwise one or two bullies
(for there are bullies even among tiny birds) are apt to
monopolise the food.

He should also bear in mind that Nature does not
provide her feathered children with teeth.   Seed-eating
birds, therefore, habitually swallow small stones and
pieces of grit.   These perform the function of millstones
inside the bird.   From this it follows that it is cruel to
keep seed-eating birds without supplying them with
sand and grit.

The bone of a cuttle-fish, tied to the wall of the cage,

is much appreciated by all the finch tribe and helps to keep them in condition.

The nest of the amadavat is a large ball of fibrous material, somewhat carelessly put together, with a hole at one side by way of entrance. Winter is the season in which to look for the nests, but they are not easy to find, being well concealed in low bushes. Six pure white glossless eggs are usually laid.

THE NUTMEG BIRD

THE nutmeg bird or spotted munia (*Uroloncha punctulata*) is second only to the amadavat as an aviary favourite. The two species are almost invariably caged together· This is, perhaps, the reason why I was once gravely assured by a lady that the spotted munia is the hen and the amadavat the cock of one and the same species! Needless to say, the birds, although relatives, belong to different genera. The stouter bill of the spotted munia proclaims this. In colour the beak is bluish black or dark slate colour, and contrasts strongly with the chocolate-brown of the head, neck, back, wings, and tail. The breast is white with a number of black rings, which give it the appearance of a nutmeg-grater, hence the popular name of the bird. Fanciers go one better and call it the spice bird. If in years to come the former name be forgotten, etymologists will put their wise heads together and puzzle and wrangle over the derivation of the name "spice bird"!

The habits of the spotted munia are those of the amadavat. Like the latter, it seems to thrive in captivity; it also loves warmth, and likes to go to roost with a warm companion on each side of it. Red and spotted munias live together very amicably in a cage; but as the latter, owing to their less showy plumage, are usually in a minority, they have to be content with outside positions at roosting-time. Sometimes my munias take it into their tiny heads to sleep on a perch which runs across a corner of the cage, and is barely long enough to accommodate them all. There are several other finer and longer perches, but, for some reason or other, they seem to prefer this one. Possibly its breadth is better adapted to the grip of their feet than that of any of the others. I may here say, in parenthesis, for the benefit of those who keep cage birds, that every cage should contain several perches of varying diameter, so as to permit the inmates of the cage the luxury of a change of grip.

Well, when a dozen birds persist in roosting on a perch intended only to seat ten, at least one of them is unable to find room on the perch, and is obliged either to sleep on the backs of some of his companions or make-believe that he is roosting on the perch. This latter feat is accomplished by the bird clutching hold of the two wires between which the perch passes and maintaining himself at an angle of 45° with the vertical. In this attitude a bird will sometimes sleep! Of course, its body is in part resting on that of its neighbour, but, allowing for this, a more uncomfortable position is inconceivable to a human being. The spotted munia, however, seems to find it tolerably comfortable.

Birds sleep standing, often on one leg. Did this require any appreciable muscular effort on the part of the bird there could be no rest in such an attitude, and the bird would fall off its perch as soon as it went to sleep. As a matter of fact, the muscles and tendons of a bird's hind-limb are so arranged that, to use the words of Mr. F. W. Headley, "when the leg bends at the ankle, there is a pull upon the tendons, the muscles are stretched, the toes are bent and grasp the perch on which the bird sits. Thus he is maintained by his own weight, which bends the leg and so causes the toes to grip." Thanks to this feature of their anatomy, passerine birds are able to sleep on branches of trees out of reach of prowling beasts of prey.

The great force with which a bird grasps its perch is worthy of note. As every hawker is aware, a falcon, when carried on the wrist, grips the leather gauntlet so tightly as to almost stop the circulation of the blood in the hand of the carrier. A fox cannot open its mouth when once its snout is in the iron grip of an eagle. Examples of the power of the grip of the foot of a passerine bird will occur to every one who has had much to do with our feathered friends. Crows habitually roost in the topmost branches of trees, which must be very violently shaken in a gale of wind ; yet the birds never seem to lose their hold.

I have said that the habits of the spotted munia are those of the amadavat ; what was said of the latter applies to the former, with one exception. The spotted munia is no songster. Those who keep the bird must have seen him go through all the motions of singing, with a considerable display of energy, but scarcely a sound seems to issue. You may perhaps hear the feeblest noise, like that made by a wheezy and decrepit mosquito. When you see the bird's mandibles

moving nineteen to the dozen with scarcely a sound
issuing, you are inclined to think that he is either playing dumb crambo or that he has taken leave of his
senses. Nothing of the kind. The bird is singing his
top notes, which are doubtless greatly appreciated by
his mate. Sound is, as we all know in this scientific age,
vibration appreciable to the ear. Air is the usual vibrating medium. Only certain vibrations are perceptible
to the human auditory organ. Those having a recurrence of below thirty or above sixteen thousand per
second do not produce the sensation of sound to the
average human ear. There are thus numbers of vibrations continually going on which are lost to us; to this
category belong the vibrations in the air produced by
the vocal cords of the spotted munia. The ear of a
bird is constituted very differently from that of man,
so that it is not surprising if birds can hear certain
sounds imperceptible to us human beings. I may here
say that the range of the human ear varies greatly in
different individuals. Some men can hear vibrations
of which the recurrence is but fifteen in the second,
while others are said to appreciate notes caused by forty
thousand vibrations per second. I have a friend who
cannot hear a black partridge when it is calling; its
notes are too high for the unusually limited range of his
ear. I do not know if there are any people to whom
the note of the nutmeg bird sounds quite loud; if
there be, and these lines meet their eye, I hope they will
give their brethren of more limited capacity the benefit
of their experience.

THE DID-HE-DO-IT

MR. "did-he-do-it" is a dandy of the first water. I should like to add "and so is his wife," for she dresses exactly as he does, and is every bit as particular regarding her personal appearance, but owing to the peculiarity of our Anglo-Saxon tongue, it is incorrect to apply the term "dandy" to a lady, and there appears to be no feminine equivalent of it. I must therefore be content to say that Mrs. Did-he-do-it is a dressy little person. Before describing the attire of the Did-he-do-it let me say that the bird is correctly styled the red-wattled lapwing. Ornithologists used to call it *Lobivanellus goensis*, but this was found to be a bit of a mouthful for even an ornithologist; accordingly the bird is now named *Sarcogrammus indicus* for short.

The Did-he-do-it belongs to the noble family of plovers. Its head, neck, and upper back are black, and the under parts are white. A broad white band runs down each side of the neck from the eye to join the white of the under parts. The wings are of a beautiful greenish-bronze hue; the legs are bright yellow. The beak is crimson-red, as is the forwardly pointing wattle which forms so conspicuous a feature of the bird's physiognomy. The lapwing is thus an easy bird to identify. Even if you cannot see him, you know he is there the moment you hear his loud, shrill " Did he do it, pity to do it." The only bird with which he can possibly be confounded is his cousin, the yellow-wattled lapwing (*Sarciophorus malabaricus*). This latter, however, has a yellow wattle and one syllable less in its cry.

The Did-he-do-it is a bird which frequents open plains in the neighbourhood of water. I have never seen it perched on a tree, and as it does not possess the luxury of a hind toe, I imagine that, like the old lady after a rough Channel crossing, it likes to feel itself on " *terra cotta.*"

This bird is not likely to be seen within municipal limits, but it is fairly abundant outside Madras. It feeds chiefly upon insects and small crustacea. It is not a gluttonous fowl. " Eha " declares that you never find it where there is food and that it does without sleep, since you never catch it napping. Jerdon, however, informs us that in the South of India it is said to sleep on its back with its legs in the air—a distinctly undignified position for a dandy. It sleeps thus so as to be able to catch on its toes the sky in case this should happen to fall down. As " Eha " says, the chief point about this truly native yarn is that it is impossible to contradict it, for who has seen a lapwing asleep?

The nesting habits of the Did-he-do-it are most interesting. Strictly speaking, it does not build a nest. It scrapes a cavity, about a quarter of an inch deep, in some stony place. This is the nest. Round it there are a few pieces of *kankar* or some twigs;

whether these are brought thither by the bird, or have merely been brushed there in the making of the cavity, I know not. Very frequently the nest is situated in the ballast of the railway line. Sometimes it is so placed that the footboard of every carriage passes over the head of the sitting bird. There is no accounting for tastes! Four eggs are usually laid; they are much more pointed at one end than at the other, and are invariably placed in the nest so as to form a star, the blunt ends projecting outwards and the thin ends nearly meeting at the centre.

Lapwings' eggs are protectively coloured. Being laid in the open and not hidden away in a nest, it is important that they should not be conspicuous, otherwise they would soon be espied and devoured by some egg-eating creature. Thus they are coloured so as to assimilate with their surroundings. The ground colour is greenish and is boldly splotched with sepia, some of the splotches being darker than others. The eggs are dull and not glossy, hence are very difficult to distinguish from the stones which lie round about them. From the above description it will be seen that the Did-he-do-it's egg is very like that of his cousin the English plover, whose eggs are held to be so great a delicacy. Why these eggs are so much esteemed I do not know. I suspect that it is because they are difficult to find, and so costly. If tripe and onions cost fifty shillings a pound, this dish would probably form the *pièce de résistance* of every millionaire's banquet.

The eggs of the Did-he-do-it, then, are interesting as forming perfect examples of protectively coloured objects. As I have previously remarked, the theory of protective colouration has my deepest sympathy. It is an unfortunate jade upon which every biologist seems to think that he is entitled to take free rides; the result is that the poor beast's ribs are cutting through its skin! For example, every bird's egg is supposed to be protectively coloured—even the gorgeous shining blue egg laid by the seven sisters, which is, in truth, about as much protectively coloured as the I Zingari Cricket Club blazer is. The majority of eggs are laid in nests which are either covered in or more or less well concealed among foliage, hence there is no necessity for them to be protectively coloured. Dame Nature is free to exercise on them to the uttermost her artistic temperament, with the result that there are few things more beautiful than a collection of birds' eggs.

So well do the eggs of the lapwing assimilate with their surroundings, that, if you would discover a clutch of them, your only chance is to watch the actions of the possessors of the nest. But the Did-he-do-it is a wily bird, and if you are not very cute he will live up to his name by "doing you in the eye." He does not, like babblers and bulbuls, make a tremendous noise as you approach the nest. He assumes a nonchalant, I might say jaunty, air, hoping thereby to put the intruder off the scent. The other day I had the pleasure of circumventing a couple of lapwings. Feeling tolerably certain that a pair had a nest on a flat piece of ground near a canal bank, I determined to find that nest. My wife accompanied me. On arriving at the spot we took cover under some trees and scanned the horizon with field-glasses, but saw no trace of a lapwing. I began to think I had made a mistake. After a time we walked on towards the canal; when we had gone some three hundred yards my wife noticed a bird on a ridge by the canal. By the aid of glasses I saw it was a Did-he-do-it. We both dropped down and watched. The bird had "spotted" us, for he had assumed the air of an old sailor who is smoking a pipe over a mug of beer, the air of a man without a care in the world. Presently he quietly disappeared behind the little ridge. We then made a big detour so as to reach the other side of this. Having arrived there we sat behind a tree. The lapwing was now eyeing us suspiciously. We affected to take no notice of him. Presently a second Did-he-do-it came out from behind a clump of low plants only to disappear into it almost immediately, and then ostentatiously reappear after a few seconds. Had we not known the wiles of the lapwing we should have located the nest behind that clump. But we knew better and waited. One of the birds again disappeared behind the clump, but emerged at the other side and strolled along very slowly; presently it came to some stones, where it stood motionless for a few seconds. It then sat down, or rather slowly sank into a sitting position. There was no doubt that the bird was now on the nest. We made for it. As we approached, the bird that was not on the nest flew off, making a noise with the object of putting us off the scent. The lapwing on the nest quietly got up and strolled off without a sound. On arriving at the place where she had been sitting we found three eggs. I took one of them for a lady who was anxious to have one. Meanwhile both birds had flown away without making any noise. Having examined the nest, we returned to our watching place. In about ten minutes the bird was again sitting quite happily. She had not missed the egg.

COBBLER OR TAILOR?

THE disagreement between the popular and the scientific name of the tailor-bird (*Orthotomus sutorius*) must, I suppose, be attributed to the fact that the average ornithologist is not learned in the Classics. I freely admit that I did not notice the discrepancy until it was pointed out to me. *Orthotomus sutorius* means, not the tailoring, but the cobbling *Orthotomus*. It was, I believe, Forester who, considerably over a century ago, gave the bird the specific name which it now possesses, or rather the allied name, *sutoria*. If he wrote this in mistake for *sartoria*, the error was a stroke of genius, since the bird should certainly be called the cobbler rather than the tailor. The so-called sewing of the nest is undoubtedly a great performance for a little bird that does not possess a workbox. Nevertheless, if the *dirzie* who squats in the verandah did not work more neatly than the tailor-bird he would soon lose his place. *Orthotomus sutorius* does not sew leaves one to another, it merely cobbles them together, much as the "boy" cobbles together the holes in his master's socks.

When last I wrote about the tailor-bird, I had honestly to admit that I did not know how the bird did its work.

My attitude towards its sewing was then that of the child who sings—

> Twinkle, twinkle, little star,
> How I wonder what you are !

To-day I can boast with the learned astronomer—

> Twinkle, twinkle, little star,
> Now we all know what you are !

for I have found out how the bird does its sewing.

Some months ago Mr. G. A. Pinto, a very keen ornithologist, informed me that a tailor-bird built regularly every year in the verandah in front of his drawing-room window. He told me that he had never thought of watching the stitching operation, and was much surprised when I informed him that, so far as I knew, no one had ever observed the complete process. He said that as the bird would undoubtedly begin building shortly, he would follow the whole process from the other side of the window. He was as good as his word. It is thanks to his patient watching that I am in a position to pen this article. Towards the end of May the hen tailor-bird began "prospecting" for a likely site, for the hen alone works at the nest, and selected a *Dracæna* plant on the left-hand side of the entrance to the verandah. One of the leaves of the plant was so curved that its terminal half was parallel with the ground. Upon this she commenced operations. The first thing she did was to make with her sharp little beak a number of punctures along each edge of the leaf. In this particular case the punctures took the form of longitudinal slits, owing to the fact that the veins of the

Dracæna leaf run longitudinally. In leaves of different texture the punctures take other shapes. Having thus prepared the leaf, she disappeared for a little and returned with a strand of cobweb. One end of this she wound round the narrow part of the leaf that separated one of the punctures from the edge ; having done this, she carried the loose end of the strand across the under surface of the leaf to a puncture on the opposite side, where she attached it to the leaf and thus drew the edges a little way together. She then proceeded to connect most of the other punctures with those opposite to them, so that the leaf took the form of a tunnel converging to a point. The under surface of the leaf formed the roof and sides of the tunnel or arch. There was no floor to this, since the edges of the leaf did not meet below, the gap between them being bridged by strands of cobweb. This was a full day's work for the little bird, and more than sufficient to disqualify her for membership in any trade union.

She next went on to line with cotton this *cul-de-sac* which she had made in the leaf. She, of course, commenced by filling the tip, and the weight of the lining soon caused the hitherto horizontal leaf to hang downwards, so that it eventually became almost vertical, with the tip pointing towards the ground. When lining the nest the bird made a number of punctures in the leaf, through which she poked the lining with her beak, the object of this being to keep the lining *in situ*. It was Mr. Pinto who first called my attention to these punctures in the body of the leaf. He informed me that he had never seen a tailor-bird's nest in which the lining did not thus project through holes in the leaf, and that when searching for such nests he always looked out for this. My subsequent observations have tended to confirm his statement.

All this time the edges of the leaf that formed the nest had been held together by the thinnest strands of cobweb, and it is a mystery how these can have stood the strain. However, before the lining was completed, the bird proceeded to strengthen them by connecting the punctures on opposite edges of the leaf with threads of cotton. Her *modus operandi* was to push one end of a thread through a puncture on one edge and the other end through a puncture on the opposite edge of the leaf. The cotton used is soft and frays easily, so that that part of it which is forced through a tiny aperture issues as a fluffy knob, which looks like a knot and is usually taken for such. As a matter of fact, the bird makes no knots; she merely forces a portion of the cotton strand through a puncture, and the silicon which enters into the composition of the leaf catches the soft, minute strands of the cotton and prevents them from slipping.

Every one must have noticed how brittle a dead leaf is. This brittleness is due to the silicon which is deposited in the epidermis of the leaf. When the leaf is green the silicon is not so obvious; it is nevertheless there. Some leaves take up more silicon than others; grasses, for example, contain so much that many will cut one's hand if roughly plucked. I imagine that the tailor-bird usually selects for her nest a leaf or leaves in which there is plenty of silicon. Thus the bird does not make a knot

F

as is popularly supposed, nor is there any necessity for her to do so. Sometimes the connecting threads of cotton are sufficiently long to admit of their being passed to and fro, in which case the bird utilises the full length.

I may mention that when the nest, the building of which I have attempted to describe, was about three parts finished, Mr. Pinto noticed that the bird had ceased to work at it. He was surprised and disappointed. He then discovered that the little builder was at work on a *Dracæna* plant on the right-hand side of the entrance to the verandah, not two yards distant from the first nest. He was much astonished at the strange behaviour of the bird, and still more so when, the next day, she had resumed work at her first nest, which she completed, leaving the second unfinished at the stage when the punctures had been made and the edges of the leaf drawn together by strands of cobweb. Presently an explanation of the bird's unusual behaviour occurred to him. His dog which, ordinarily, is chained up at one end of the verandah, was, on the day the tailor-bird left her first nest, fastened up in the middle of the verandah, so that the bird while working at her nest would be within its reach. She evidently objected to this, so began a new nest; but next day, when the dog had been removed, she returned to her more advanced nursery. This accident of chaining up the dog for one day in the middle of the verandah was particularly fortunate, for it enabled me to examine carefully a nest in an early state of construction.

This account must, I fear, close with a tragedy.

When the little cobbler had been sitting on her eggs for about ten days one of the garden coolies broke them, out of mischief, and thought he had done a clever thing. He is now a sadder if not a wiser rascal!

A CROW IN COLOURS

From bough to bough the restless magpie roves,
And chatters as she flies.

THE magpie has been well called a crow in gay attire. The two species are related, and, as regards character, they are "birds of a feather." Both are bold, bad creatures, both rogues, thieves, and villains, and, as such, both appeal to me. The magpie with which we are familiar in England can scarcely be called an Indian bird. It does disport itself in happy Kashmir, and has been seen in the uninviting tract of land over which the Khan of Khelat presides. But India, as defined in the Income Tax Act, extends neither to Kashmir nor to Baluchistan, hence *Pica rustica* may decline to be considered an Indian subject. In this land of many trials his place is taken by his cousins the tree-pies. One of these— the Indian tree-pie (*Dendrocita rufa*)—is distributed throughout the plains of India, at least, so the books tell us. As a matter of fact, I have never seen the bird in or about Madras. This is curious, for Madras is a garden city (I speak not of Georgetown), and the bird ought to revel in the well-wooded compounds which beautify the capital of the Southern Presidency. Lest its absence from Madras

68

be attributed to the profession tax, let me say that the best legal authorities are of opinion that the bird would not be liable to pay the tax. Not that it would make any difference if the bird were liable. If I know him aright, he would say to the importunate tax collector, "Go and get your hair cut," or words to that effect. Nor is there, so far as I can see, anything in the much-abused climate of Madras to frighten away the bird. Perhaps the doves are too much for him. If there be one thing more than another calculated to disturb the easily upset equilibrium of the gentle dove it is the sight of a tree-pie. In those places where it occurs you may, any day of the week, see one of these long-tailed rascals being pursued and buffeted by a pair of irate and hysterically screaming doves. In this particular case the doves have some excuse for their anger. The tree-pie, or the Indian magpie as Jerdon calls him, is, to use a colloquialism, dead-nuts on a new-laid egg for his breakfast, and, as doves always display their oological productions on a shakedown in a tree, and as I defy even a museum ornithologist to discover any trace of protective colouration about the aforesaid oological treasures, we cannot be surprised if the tree-pie thinks that doves lay eggs for his especial benefit. Even if the tree-pie does not happen to have been breakfasting off their eggs the doves have ample excuse for chastising him, for does not tradition tell us that Noah's curse is upon the bird? The rascal flatly refused to enter the Ark with the other birds, so that the Patriarch had actually to send Japhet to catch it !

Unfortunately, the tree-pie does not draw the line

at eggs. It is said that it makes no bones about devouring a young bird. I have never seen the creature commit this enormity, but Jerdon is my authority for the fact that " Mr. Smith" has known a bird to enter a covered verandah of a house and nip off half a dozen young geraniums, visit a cage of small birds, begin by stealing the grain, and end by killing and eating the birds, and repeating these visits daily until destroyed. *Facilis est descensus Averni.*

This is only one side of the bird's character. I have seen a tree-pie literally obey the Biblical doctrine of turning the smitten cheek to the smiter ; nor, so far as I know, did it, like the well-brought-up boy, after having allowed its second cheek to be smitten, take off its coat and thrash the smiter. The bird in question sat motionless on a branch with a seraphic smile on its face, and appeared to be ignorant of the fact that two little furies, in the shape of fantailed flycatchers, were making puny pecks at its plumage.

But before discoursing further upon the merits and demerits of our crow in colours, let me describe him. What applies to him applies to her. To the human eye there is no external difference between the two sexes. This by way of introduction. The tree-pie is a foot and a half long, one foot being tail and the remaining inches body. The head, neck, and breast are sooty brown, and the greater part of the remaining plumage is reddish fawn. The wings are brown and silver-grey. The tail is ashy grey broadly tipped with black. It is impossible to mistake a tree-pie ; there is no other bird like it. Its flight is very characteristic, consisting of half a dozen rapid flaps of the wing followed by a little sail. The two middle tail feathers are much longer than the others, the pair next to the middle ones are the second longest, and the outer ones shortest of all. The bird, like all others, spreads out its tail during flight, and the expanded tail gives it a curious appearance.

The Indian tree-pie, as its name implies, dwells principally in trees, and spends most of its time in picking insects off the leaves and branches. When fruit is in season, it feeds largely on that. It moves with great agility from branch to branch, but it frequently descends to the ground to feed and drink. It does not, I think, ever accompany cattle, as does our poor, persecuted magpie at home. It is a sociable bird and is frequently seen in little companies of six or seven.

Like all socially inclined birds, it is very conversational. It has a great variety of notes, many of which are harsh and angry-sounding, others are whistling, metallic calls, acceptable to the human ear. The commonest of these sounds something like *coch-lee, coch-lee*. If, in a place where magpies abound, you hear any new and strange cry, you are tolerably safe in attributing it to one of those birds.

The Indian pie is not so expert a nest-builder as its European cousin. This latter, it will be remembered, builds a large domed structure of prickly twigs with an entrance at one side, well protected by thorns. I have not been able to discover why this bird is at such pains to protect the entrance to its nursery. It is so aggressive and pugnacious that no sane thing in feathers would dream of attempting to rob its nest. One ornithologist has put forth the brilliant suggestion that the protection is against its brother magpies. I cannot accept this, for I take it as an axiom that where one magpie can enter, there can another. We must also bear in mind that the Indian species manage to thrive very well in spite of their roofless nests.

UP-TO-DATE SPECIES MAKING

THE ornithological world is peopled by two classes of human beings. There are those who study nature inside the museum with the microscope and the scalpel; and there are those who love to observe birds in the open and study their habits. The former, if kept in their place, perform a very useful function, for they co-ordinate and elaborate the observations of the field naturalist. They should be most useful servants to him. Unfortunately these museum men are growing very powerful, and, like trade unions, are beginning to dictate to their masters. Indeed, they bid fair to become the masters and turn the field naturalists into their slaves. The chief aim of the arm-chair or museum ornithologist appears to be the multiplication of new species. Nowadays more species seem to be brought into being by these men than by natural selection. When they are not manufacturing new species, they are tampering with those that already exist.

I have repeatedly had occasion to speak of the marvellous, kaleidoscopic changes undergone by ornithological terminology—changes which are the despair of the field naturalist. I am not a statistician, but at a rough guess I should say that every species of bird has its name changed about once in each decade. The object of having a classical terminology is that naturalists of all countries shall have a common name for every bird and beast, and thus not be at cross-purposes when conversing or corresponding. But this object is most successfully defeated when the classical name is continually undergoing alteration. It is practically impossible for any one but the professional ornithologist to keep pace with these changes. A poor dilettante like myself has not a look in. For example, I received by the last mail * the latest issue of the Avicultural Society's Magazine and noticed in it an article on the collared turtle-dove of Burma. Wondering what this bird might be, I looked at its scientific name and found it to be *Turtur decaocta*. I looked this up in both Jerdon and the *Fauna of British India*, but could not find it ; nor could I see any mention of the collared turtle-dove. On reading through the paper I found, to my astonishment, that the bird referred to was our familiar friend the common or garden Indian ring-dove, which for years has been called *Turtur risorius*. *Risorius* was a name good enough for Jerdon, Hume, Vidal, Legge, Barnes, Reid, Davison, and a hundred other good ornithologists ; but because, forsooth, one Salvadori would like a change, we shall, I suppose, be obliged to adopt the latest new-fangled appellation.

The museum ornithologist has yet another craze. He sees that there must be some limit to the present multiplication of species, so he has hit upon the brilliant idea of making sub-species. Just as the inhabitants of

* Written towards the end of 1906.

every town and village have little local peculiarities, so have birds of the same species which live in different provinces. The latest idea is to make each of these a different sub-species with a special name of its own. In the near future the scientific name of every bird will be composed of three parts, the generic, the specific, and the sub-specific. Thus Mr. T. H. Newman has discovered that the skin round the eye of the ring-dove of Burma is not whitish, as it is in India, but yellow ; Mr. Newman therefore manufactures a new sub-species, which he calls *Turtur decaocta xanthocyclus* as opposed to the Indian bird which he calls *Turtur decaocta douraca.* We may consider ourselves lucky that he has not made a new species of the Burmese bird !

This is not an isolated case. Almost every unfortunate species in the universe is being split up into a dozen or more sub-species. Any local variation in the colour of the plumage is considered sufficient justification for the formation of a sub-species, and we shall undoubtedly, ere long, hear of sub-sub-species ! !

The hopeless thing is that any Juggins can make new sub-species. It is as easy as falling out of a tree. Let me show how it is done. Take the common sparrow. This pushing little bird, this " feathered Hooligan," as Mr. Finn calls him, is found all over the world, and every one is able to recognise the sparrow wherever he meets him as the same bird that insults people in London. But the sparrows of each country have their little peculiarities. For example, the cock sparrow in India has more white on his neck than his brother in

England.   Hence we may make a sub-species of the Indian bird and call him *Passer domesticus indicus*.

Now, close and patient observation during a prolonged sojourn in Madras has convinced me that the sparrow in the Southern Presidency (I will no longer call it the Benighted Presidency, for experience has shown me that there are other parts of India far more benighted) is quite twenty per cent. more impudent than the sparrows in Northern India.   Hence we have no option but to make a sub-sub-species of him.   Let us call him *Passer domesticus indicus maderaspatensis*. We may go even a step further.   The sparrows that hold chorus along the ledges of the iron rafters of the Connemara Hotel are far more insulting and exasperating than any other sparrows I have set eyes upon. This surely is quite sufficient provocation for making a sub-sub-sub-species of those birds.   I propose to call them *Passer domesticus indicus maderaspatensis connemara hotelwalla*—a name which I am sure will be received with acclamation both by sparrows and human beings.

But enough of this foolery.   The multiplication of species is really a very serious matter, for it is likely to deter sane persons from taking up the most delightful of studies.   If the ornithological societies of every country in the world would combine to suppress the evil, it could easily be put down.   But there is, I fear, no likelihood of such combination, because these societies are composed mostly of museum ornithologists, and it is too much to expect of these men that they will voluntarily suppress their chief enjoyment in life.   To persuade them to act in this altruistic manner it will be necessary to offer them a *quid pro quo*. The only *quid* that suggests itself to me is to invite each of them to name a bird after himself. Let the name of every known species (I mean proper and indisputable species) be put in a hat and let each member draw one out. The bird he draws will henceforth be called after him. If any birds are left undrawn after every man has shed his name on one species, the remainder could be balloted for, and thus some lucky dogs would be able to give their name to two birds. When this is once done, it should be made an offence punishable with death to change the specific name of any feathered thing. Newly discovered birds and beasts could, as heretofore, be named after the happy discoverer. This proposal will, if adopted, cure the evil. My point is that it does not matter a jot what a bird be called ; the important thing is to give it a fixed and immutable name, so that we poor field naturalists shall know where we are.

HONEYSUCKERS

HONEYSUCKERS are birds that have adopted the manner of living of the butter-fly, and a charming mode of life it is. To flit about in the sunshine and drink sweet draughts of the nectar that lies hidden away at the base of the petals of flowers is indeed an idyllic existence.

The sunbird, as the honeysucker is frequently called, is provided with a curved beak and a long tubular tongue to enable it the better to rob cup-like blossoms of their honey. The bird must perforce be very small and light, or it would find it impossible to reach the nectar of many flowers. As a matter of fact, it is almost as light as air, so is able to support itself on one flower when drinking honey from another. Sometimes, if no perch be available, the little honeysucker will hover in the air on rapidly vibrating wings and thus extract the sweets from a flower. In this attitude it looks very like a butterfly. I may here mention that sunbirds do not live exclusively upon honey: they vary this diet with minute insects which they pick off flowers and leaves.

Honeysuckers are frequently called humming-birds by Anglo-Indians. This is not correct. Humming-birds are confined to the New World, and are smaller

LOTEN'S SUNBIRD. (ARACHNEC-THRA LOTENIA)
(Note the long curved bill, adapted to insertion in flowers)

and more ethereal than our little honeysuckers, but their methods of feeding are so similar that the mistake is a pardonable one.

As every one knows, butterflies and bees, in return for the honey they receive, render service to the flowers by carrying the pollen from the stamen of one to the stigma of the other and thus bring about cross-fertilisation, which most botanists believe to be essential to the well-being of a species. Honeysuckers probably perform a similar service, for, as they flit from flower to flower, their little heads may be seen to be well dusted with yellow pollen.

Sunbirds are found all over India, but they are most plentiful in the South, being essentially tropical birds; they are merely summer visitors to the Punjab; when the short, cold winter days come, they leave that province and betake themselves to some milder clime.

Three species may be seen in our Madras gardens— Loten's, the purple, and the yellow honeysucker.

Of the cocks of the first and second species (*Arachnechthra lotenia* and *A. asiatica*) it may perhaps be said that they are clothed in purple and fine linen, for their plumage is a deep, rich purple with a sheen and a gloss like that on a brand-new silk hat. Sometimes the bird looks black, at others green, and more frequently mauve, according to the intensity of the light and the angle at which the sun's rays fall upon it. It is not very easy to distinguish between these two sunbirds unless specimens are held in the hand, when the violet-black abdomen of the purple species can be easily distinguished from the snuff-brown lower parts of

Loten's. However, the latter has a much longer and stouter beak, and is very abundant in Madras, while the purple bird is comparatively rare, so that the Madrassi is fairly safe in setting down all the purple birds he sees as Loten's honeysuckers. If, however, he espies a purple sunbird, with an unusually short bill, a bird that sings like a canary, he may be certain that that particular one is *A. asiatica*. If the cock Loten's sunbird is clothed in purple and fine linen, that of the yellow species (*A. zeylonica*) may be said to be arrayed in a coat of many colours, each of which is so beautiful as to defy imitation by the painter. There is a patch on the crown which appears metallic lilac in some lights and emerald-green in others. His neck and upper back are dull crimson, the lower back, chin, and throat are brilliant metallic purple. The tail and wing feathers are dark brown. There is a maroon collar below the throat, and the plumage from this collar downwards is bright yellow. Verily, Solomon in all his glory was not arrayed like one of these.

The hens of all three species are homely-looking birds, difficult to distinguish one from the other. The upper plumage of each is dingy brown and the lower parts dull yellow. Many ornithologists declare that sexual dimorphism, such as is here displayed, is due to the greater need of the hen for protection when sitting on the eggs. These people allege that if the hens of brightly plumaged species were as showy as the cocks, they would be conspicuous objects when brooding, and so fall easy victims to birds of prey. This is a theory typical of the arm-chair naturalist, or of him who studies

THE YELLOW SUNBIRD. (ARACHNEC-THRA ZEYLONICA)

nature through the grimy panes of a museum window. Like all such theories, it is tempting at first sight, but is untenable because it fails to take cognisance of facts with which every field-naturalist should be acquainted. In the first place, birds of prey rarely attack stationary objects : they look out for moving quarry. Secondly, the cock of many species, such as the paradise flycatcher (*Terpsiphone paradisi*), although he is far more showy than the hen, sits on the eggs in the open nest quite as much as she does. In this case what is sauce for the goose is sauce for the gander; if she needs protective colouring, so does he. It is true that the cock sunbird never takes a turn on the nest; he is not a family man, but a gay young spark, who goes about bravely attired, with his hand upon the handle of his sword, ready to draw it upon the least provocation. A more pugnacious little bird does not exist. While the hen is laboriously building the wonderful little nest, he spends his time in drinking and revelry, with an occasional visit to the growing nursery to criticise its construction. Hence it might seem that, in the case of the sunbird, the above-mentioned explanation of the sexual dimorphism is the true one. Unfortunately, the nest is not an open one, but a little mango-shaped structure with an entrance at the side, so that the hen when sitting in it is not visible from above. In this case, therefore, as in so many others, we must seek a new explanation of this difference in the appearance of the cocks and hens.

The nest is in shape and size like a mango. It hangs down from the end of a branch, or any other convenient object. It is composed of dried grass,

G

leaves, cocoons, bits of paper, and any kind of rubbish, held together by means of cobweb and some glutinous substance. There is an entrance at the side, over which is a little porch that serves to keep out rain and sun, but this porch is seen in every nest, even when the bird builds, as it very frequently does, in a verandah. A sunbird recently made its nest in the verandah of a friend of mine; the latter came to me and expressed his contempt for the intellect of the little architect, since she had been fool enough to construct a porch, although the nest was built under cover. He forgot that the building of nests is largely an instinctive act, that each bird builds on a fixed plan, learned by it in "the school of the woods."

The nest is cosily lined with cotton down. No attempt is made to conceal it; nevertheless it frequently escapes the notice of human beings, because it does not look like a nest; one is apt to mistake it for a mass of dried grass and rubbish that has become caught in a branch. A sunbird in my compound completely covered her nest with the paper shavings that had once formed the packing for a tin of biscuits. The *khansamah*, when opening the tin, had, after the manner of his kind, pitched the shavings out of the window of the cookhouse.

It is doubtful whether predacious creatures mistake the sunbird's nest for a mass of rubbish; but it is so well placed that they cannot get at it. It is invariably situated sufficiently far above the ground to be out of reach of a four-legged animal; it hangs from an outstanding branch so that no crow or kite can get a

NEST OF LOTEN'S SUNBIRD
(Notice that it is built in a spider's web)

foothold anywhere near it, and the squirrel who ventured to trust himself on to the nest would, I believe, look very foolish when attacked by the owners.

As is usually the case with birds that build covered nests, the hen is not at all shy. If her nursery happens to be in a verandah, she will sit in it with her head out of the window, and watch with interest the owners of the bungalow taking afternoon tea three feet below her.

A HEWER OF WOOD

NOT the least of the many benefits which birds confer upon man is the unceasing warfare which the majority of them wage upon insects. Insects may be said to dominate the earth; they fill every nook and cranny of it, preying upon all other living things which they outnumber. If this is the state of affairs when hundreds of millions of insects are devoured daily by their arch-foes, the fowls of the air, what would it be were there no birds? The earth would certainly not be inhabited by men.

Most insectivorous birds specialise, that is to say, lay themselves out to catch a particular class of insect. Swifts, swallows, and flycatchers have developed phenomenal mastery over the air, so prey upon flying insects. Mynas, hoopoes, "blue jays," magpie-robins, and others feed upon the hexapod hosts that crawl on the ground. Not a few birds confine their attention to the creeping things that inhabit the bark of trees. Such are the wryneck, the tree-creeper, and the woodpecker. Of these the woodpecker is chief. A mighty insect hunter is he, one who tracks down his quarry and drags him out of his lair. How must the insects which lie hidden away in the crevices of the bark tremble as they hear this feathered Nimrod battering at the walls of their citadel!

No bird is better adapted than the woodpecker to the work which nature has given him. He is a perfect hunting machine, constructed for work in trees. Note the ease with which he moves over the upright trunk. His sharp claws can obtain a foothold on almost any surface. I have seen a golden-backed woodpecker hunting insects on a smooth well-wheel!

His tail, which is short and composed of very stiff feathers, acts almost like a third leg. The bristle-like feathers stick in the crevices of the bark and enable the bird to maintain his position while he hammers away with might and main. His head is his hammer and his beak his chisel. The chisel is fixed rigidly in the hammer so that none of the force of the blow is lost. It is exhilarating to watch a woodpecker at work. He stands with his legs wide apart, the tip of his tail pressed firmly against the bark, and puts all he knows into each stroke, drawing his head back as far as it will go and then letting drive. The manner in which his strokes follow one another puts me in mind of the clever way in which workmen drive an iron bar into a macadamised road by raining upon it blows with sledge-hammers. Almost before the hammer of the first striker is off the head of the bar the second has struck it, this is immediately followed by the hammer of the third, then, without a pause, the first hammerer gets his second blow home, and so they continue until a halt is called. As a small boy I would stand for hours watching the operation. I am ashamed to do so now, so have to content myself with observing woodpeckers at work! There are few things more fascinating to watch than an operation in which skill and brute force are deftly combined.

Even more useful than the beak as a weapon is the woodpecker's tongue. This is such an important organ that its owner is known in some parts of England as the tongue bird. It is so long that there is a special apparatus at the back of the bird's head for stowing it away. Its surface is studded with backwardly pointing bristles and the whole covered with sticky saliva. When the woodpecker espies a crack in the bark it inserts into it the long ribbon-like tongue. To this the luckless insects stick and are ruthlessly dragged out to their doom.

The commonest woodpecker in India is the beautiful golden-backed species (*Brachypternus aurantius*). The head and crest of the cock are bright crimson, the upper back is a beautiful golden yellow, hence the popular name of the bird. The lower back and tail are black; the wing feathers are black and golden yellow, spotted with white, and the sides of the head show a white background on which there is a network of black lines and streaks.

The hen differs from the cock in having the top of the head black with small white triangular spots.

The golden-backed woodpecker is one of our noisiest birds. It constantly utters its loud screaming call, which is similar to that of the white-breasted kingfisher. Its flight, like that of most, if not all woodpeckers, is laborious and noisy, the whir of its wings being audible at a considerable distance. The bird gives one or two vigorous flaps of its wings and thus moves in an upward direction, then it sails and sinks; a few more flaps again send it upwards, and so it continues until it reaches the tree trunk for which it is bound.

I do not think that the woodpecker ever takes a sustained flight. It is seen at its best when on the stem of a tree, over which it moves with wonderful ease in a series of silent jerks, like a mechanical toy. It always keeps its head pointing heavenwards and hops or jerks itself upwards, downwards, or sideways, with equal ease, just as though it went by clockwork. It sometimes ventures on the ground, from which it digs out insects. On the earth it progresses in the same jerky manner.

I have never seen a woodpecker sitting like an ordinary bird on a perch. It is often seen on branches, but always lengthwise, never sitting across the branch. It can move along the under surface of a horizontal bough as easily as a fly walks on the ceiling.

I sometimes wonder how woodpeckers roost. Do they sleep hanging on to the trunk of some tree, do they sit lengthwise on a branch as a nightjar does, or do they repair to some hole? I should be inclined to favour the last of these alternatives but for the fact that woodpeckers seem to excavate a new nest every year. This would not be necessary if each bird had a hole in which it slept at night.

Sometimes the bird digs out the whole of its nest, but this is not usual. The woodpecker belongs to the "labouring classes," and, true to the traditions of its caste, it is averse to work, so generally utilises a ready-made cavity. It taps away at tree after tree until it comes upon a place in a trunk that sounds hollow; it then proceeds to excavate a neat, round passage leading to this hollow. In this ready-made cavity it deposits its white eggs, not troubling to add any lining to the nesting chamber.

Woodpeckers in England suffer much at the hands of rascally starlings. These latter nest in holes, but not of their own making. If they cannot find any ready-made hollow they listen for the hammering of a woodpecker. They wait until he has completed the nest, and then take possession while his back is turned. When the rightful owner returns the starling looks out of the entrance with finely simulated indignation and asks the woodpecker what he means by intruding. In vain does the latter expostulate. *J'y suis, j'y reste* is the attitude of the starling. The result is that our feathered carpenter, not being over-valorous, retires and proceeds to hew out another nest. Woodpeckers in India do not suffer such treatment, for starlings do not breed in this country. Their cousins, the mynas, are not so impudent. The only Indian birds which nest in holes, and have sufficient impudence to eject a woodpecker, are the green parrots; but these breed in January, so that their family cares for the year are over long before the woodpecker begins nest building.

A FEATHERED SPRINTER

WHICH is the most difficult bird to shoot?
You may put this question to a dozen
sportsmen; probably no two will name
the same bird, and each will be able to
give excellent reasons why the particular fowl he mentions is the hardest to hit. The reason for this diversity
of opinion is simply that there exists no bird more
difficult to shoot than all others. Even as beauty is
said to be in the eye of the beholder, so does the difficulty, or otherwise, of shooting any particular species
depend upon the idiosyncrasies of the would-be slayer.
To some shooters all birds, with the possible exception
of the coot, are difficult to bring down, while others are
able to make every flying thing appear an easy mark.

To my way of thinking the chukor (*Caccabis chucar*)
takes a lot of hitting, but this species receives much
help on account of its mountainous habitat. It is difficult to hit even a hoary old peacock if the bird gets up
when you, already pumped to exhaustion by a stiff
climb, are engaged in scrambling from one terraced
field to another with your gun at "safe." The chukor,
thanks to the fact, conclusively proved by our friend
Euclid, that any two sides of a triangle are greater
than the third, enjoys so great an advantage over the

wingless *shikari* that it would be a contemptible creature
were it not difficult to shoot. Were I the leader of a
covey of chukor, I should thoroughly enjoy an attempt
to shoot me. Having taken up a strategic position
near the summit of a steep hill, I should squat there in
full view until the sportsman had by laborious effort
climbed to a spot some hundred and twenty yards from
where I was sitting ; I should then gracefully retire with
my retinue across the *khud* to the opposite hill, and
watch with interest the shooter clamber down one
limb of an isosceles triangle and swarm up the other.
Some time before he had completed the operation I
should again proceed to give him a practical demonstra-
tion of the fact that the base of certain triangles is considerably shorter than the sum of the other two sides.

If you take away from the chukor his natural ad-
vantages I am inclined to think that the grey partridge
(*Francolinus pondicerianus*) is the more difficult bird to
shoot. This species is common in most parts of India,
yet I do not remember ever having heard of any one
making a big bag of grey partridge. Some there are
who say that the bird is not worth shooting. If these
good folk mean that the shooting of the partridge involves so large an expenditure of ammunition as to
deter them from the undertaking I am inclined to agree
with them. Given a fair field in the shape of a plain
well studded with prickly pear, there is, in my opinion,
no bird more difficult to hit than the grey partridge. It
is, like all game birds proper, a very rapid flier for a
short distance. But it is not so much this which makes
it hard to shoot as the rapidity with which it can run

LOTEN'S SUNBIRD (HEN) ABOUT TO ENTER NEST

along the ground and the close manner in which it lies up. According to Mr. Lockwood Kipling, the grey partridge, as it runs, "suggests a graceful girl tripping along with a full skirt well held up." In a sense the simile is a good one, for the lower plumage of the partridge is curiously "full," and so does make the bird look as though it were holding up its skirts. But until graceful young ladies are able to gather up their ample skirts and sprint the "hundred" two or three yards inside "level time," it will be inaccurate to compare the tripping gait of the one to the speedy motion of the other. The grey partridge is a winged sprinter, a feathered Camilla. It can for a short distance hold its own comfortably against a galloping horse. Frequently have I come upon a covey, feeding in the open and giving vent to the familiar call, and have immediately proceeded to stalk it in the hopes of obtaining a couple of good shots. Before getting within range, one of the birds invariably "spots" me and gives the alarm. The calling immediately ceases and the partridges walk briskly to cover. The instant they disappear I dash towards the cover, hoping to surprise and flush them, but they run three yards to my two, and by the time I reach the bushes into which they betook themselves they are laughing at me from afar.

Then the way in which a partridge will sometimes lie up in comparatively thin cover is remarkable. One day, when shooting snipe at sunrise, I surprised a partridge feeding in a field. I fired, but apparently did not hit the bird, for it disappeared into a clump of palm trees and prickly pear. Taking up a position close to this clump, I instructed my beaters to throw stones into it. This they did, but half a dozen stones, to say nothing of as many chunks of clay and the most frantic yells and shouts, elicited no response from the partridge. I therefore moved on, and the moment I had turned my back on the clump the bird flew out! This is typical of my experience as a partridge shooter; the birds almost invariably get up from cover at a moment when I cannot possibly take a shot at them. Well might I sing with Cowper—

> I stride o'er the stubble each day with my gun
> Never ready to shoot till the covey is flown.

For these reasons partridge shooting is to me a particularly exasperating form of sport. There are few things more annoying than to hear—"the partridge burst away on whirring wings," from a bush on which you have just turned your back after having thrown into it half the contents of a ploughed field!

I am not a bloodthirsty individual, and enjoy watching birds through a field-glass quite as much as, if not more than, shooting them with a gun, but there is something in the call of the grey partridge which makes me want to shoot him. His shrill "pateela, pateela, pateela," seems to be a challenge. Grahame sings—

> Cheerily
> The partridge now her tuneless call repeats.

For "cheerily" write "cheekily" and you have a good description of the call of our Indian grey partridge, which may be heard in Madras every morning during the winter months.

This bird does not build an elaborate nest. There is no necessity for it to do so. A nest is a nursery in which young birds are for a time sheltered from the dangers that beset them in the world. When they have developed sufficiently to be able to look after themselves they leave the nest.

It is one of the characteristics of the gallinaceous family of birds, which includes grouse, poultry, pea- and guinea-fowl, pheasants, turkeys, and quail, that their young are able to run about almost immediately after issuing from the egg. They are born covered with down, and are thus at first very unlike their parents. They are in reality larvæ, that is to say, embryonic forms which are able to fend for themselves with little or no assistance from their parents. They change into the adult form, not hidden away in a nursery, but in the open world.

The nest, then, of the partridge is a very insignificant affair. It is usually a depression in the ground, so shallow as to be barely perceptible, and always well concealed in a bush or tuft of grass. Sometimes the eggs are laid on the bare soil, but more usually the depression is lined with grass or leaves. Occasionally the lining is so thick as to form a regular pad. From six to nine whitish eggs are laid. These do not match the ground or material on which they lie, hence cannot be considered as examples of protective colouring. Their safety depends on the fact that they are hidden away under a bush or tuft of grass. The hen, too, is a very close sitter, and her plumage assimilates well with the surroundings of the nest.

A BIRD OF CHARACTER

I HAVE hinted more than once at the possibility of there being some understanding between the architect of my bungalow and the feathered folk. On this hypothesis alone am I able to account for the presence of a rectangular hole in the porch, about eight feet above the level of the ground, a hole caused by the deliberate omission of one or two bricks. The scramble for this cavity by those species of birds which build in holes is as great as that of Europeans to secure bungalows in a Presidency town. Last year a pair of spotted owlets (*Athene brama*) secured the prize and reared up a noisy brood of four. These were regarded with mingled feelings by the human inhabitants of the bungalow. On the one hand, a bird more amusing than the clownish little owlet does not exist, on the other, it is excessively noisy. Each member of the family talks gibberish at the top of its voice, sixteen to the dozen, and as all will persist in speaking at once, the result is a nocturnal chorus that will bear comparison with the efforts of the cats which enliven the Londoner's back yard.

This year a couple of mynas (*Acridotheres tristis*) secured the highly desirable nesting site. Immediately on entering into possession they proceeded to cover the

THE INDIAN SPOTTED OWLET. (ATHENE BRAMA)

floor of the cavity with a collection of rubbish, composed chiefly of rags, grass, twigs, and bits of paper. There was no attempt at arranging this rubbish, it was bundled pell-mell into the hole and four pretty blue eggs were laid on top of it.

One might suppose that the more intelligent the bird the greater the degree of architectural skill it would display. This, however, is not the case. Were it so, crows, mynas, and parrots would build palatial nests.

Mynas do not always nestle in holes in buildings; they are content with any kind of a cavity, whether it be in a building, a tree, or a sandbank. In default of a hole they are content with a ledge, provided it be covered with a roof. A few years ago a pair of mynas reared up a brood on a ledge in the much-frequented verandah of the Deputy Commissioner's Court at Fyzabad.

To return to the nest in my porch. The eggs in due course gave rise to four nestlings of the ordinary ugly, triangular-mouthed, alderman-stomached variety. When they were nearly ready to leave the nest I took away two of them by way of rent for the use of my bungalow. This action was in complete accord with oriental custom. In India the landlord has, from time immemorial, taken from his tenants a portion of their produce as rent or land revenue. The Congress will doubtless declare that in levying 50 per cent. of the family brood I assessed the family too highly; but I defy even a Bengali orator to take 33 per cent. of four young mynas. I might, it is true, have assessed the rent at 25 per cent., but the life of a solitary myna cannot be a very happy one, so I took two, a cock and a hen.

To the ordinary observer the cock myna is as like the hen as one pea is like any other pea. To one, however, who has an eye for such things, the bigger head and more massive body of the cock render him easily recognisable when in company with his sisters. The brood consisted of two cocks and two hens, so that I made a fair division. Some there are who may question the ethics of my action. I would remind such that, incredible as it may seem, the parent birds, in all probability, did not miss the two young ones. Birds cannot count. Even the wily crow is unable to "spot" the extra egg which the koel has surreptitiously introduced into the nest. It is, of course, possible that although those mynas could not count, they missed the two young birds to the extent of noticing that something was wrong with their brood. If they did all I can say is that they concealed their feelings in an admirable manner, for they continued to feed the remaining young as though nothing had happened. If it be thought incredible that the young birds were not missed, is it not equally hard to believe that not one of the lower animals can tell the difference between two and three? If a dog has three bones before him and you remove one of them, he will not miss it unless he sees you remove it!

A *chaprassi* was appointed to nurse my two young mynas, with instructions to keep them until they should become somewhat more presentable. At the end of three weeks they were adjudged fit to appear in public, being somewhat smaller and rather lanky editions of their parents, with the patch behind the eye white instead of yellow. Having been taken from the nest they were perfectly tame, showing no fear of man, and readily accepting food from the hand.

Young nestlings display no fear of man, and do not appear to mind being handled by a human being; but as they grow older they learn to fear all strange creatures, hence it is that captive birds taken from the nest are always tamer than those which are caught after they are fledged. It was amusing to see the way in which my young mynas ran towards the *chaprassi* when he called " Puppy, puppy." " Puppy " is apparently a term applied by native servants indiscriminately to any kind of pet kept by a *sahib*.

Mynas make excellent pets because they are so alert and vivacious, and, above all, because they have so much character.

A myna is a self-assertive bird, a bird that will stand no nonsense.

I know of few things more amusing than to witness a pair of mynas give a snake a bit of their minds as they waltz along beside it in a most daring manner.

Owing to the self-assertion of the myna he is apt to be quarrelsome.

Street brawls are, I regret to say, by no means uncommon. In these two or three mynas attack one another so fiercely that they get locked together and roll over and over—a swearing, struggling ball of brown, yellow, and white.

The myna, although by no means a songster, is able to emit a great variety of notes, all of which must be familiar to every Anglo-Indian.

A bird which can produce a large number of sounds

H

is almost invariably a good mimic, and the common myna is no exception to this rule. In this respect, however, he does not compare favourably with the grackles or hill-mynas, as they are commonly called. These can imitate any sound, from the crack of a whip and the exhortations of a bullock-cart driver to the throat-clearing operation in which our Indian brethren so frequently indulge.

SWIFTS

S WIFTS are extraordinary birds; there are no others like unto them; they are the most mysterious of the many mysterious products of natural selection; their athletic feats transcend the descriptive powers of the English language. What adjective is there of suitable application to a bird that speeds through the air without an appreciable effort at the rate of a hundred miles an hour, that traverses a thousand miles every day of its existence?

These wonderful birds are everywhere common, yet much of their life history requires elucidation.

Probably not one man in fifty is able to distinguish between a swallow and a swift. Some think that "swift" and "swallow" are synonymous terms, while others believe that a swift is a kind of black swallow. As a matter of fact, the swift differs more widely from the swallow than the crow does from the canary. There is, it is true, a very strong professional likeness between the swift and the swallow, but this likeness is purely superficial ; it is merely the resemblance engendered by similar modes of obtaining a livelihood. Both swallows and swifts feed exclusively on minute insects which they catch upon the wing, hence both have a large gape, light, slender bodies, and long, powerful wings. But speedy though it be, the swallow is not in the same

99

class with the swift as a flyer. When both birds are
in the hand nothing is easier than to tell a swift from
a swallow or a martin. The latter have the ordinary
passerine foot, which consists of three forwardly directed
toes and a backwardly directed one. This foot enables
a bird to perch, so that one frequently sees swallows
seated on telegraph wires. But one never sees a swift
on a perch, because all its four toes point forward. It
cannot even walk. It spends its life in the air. It eats
and drinks on the wing, it does everything, except
sleeping and incubating, in the air.

But it is not often that one has a swallow or swift
in the hand; it is difficult to get near enough to them
to put salt on the tail, so that it is necessary to have
some means of distinguishing them when sailing through
the air. There is a very marked difference in the manner
in which these birds use their wings. This is inimitably
described by Mr. E. H. Aitken: "As a swallow darts
along, its wings almost close against its sides at every
stroke, and it looks like a pair of scissors opening and
shutting. Now a swift never closes its wings in this
way. It whips the air rapidly with the points of them,
but they are always extended and evenly curved from
tip to tip like a bow, the slim body of the bird being the
arrow." As a swift speeds through the air it looks something like an anchor, with a short shaft and enormous
flukes. If this be borne in mind, it is scarcely possible
to mistake a swift for a swallow. Swifts are abundant in
Calcutta, but one is not likely to come across a swallow
there except when the moon happens to be blue.

The two swifts commonly seen in Calcutta are the

Indian swift (*Cypselus affinis*) and the palm swift (*C. batassiensis*).

The latter need not detain us long. It is a small and weak edition of the former. It builds a cup-shaped nest on the under side of the great fan-like leaves of the toddy palm.

The Indian swift is, in size and appearance, much like the swift which visits England every summer, except for the fact that it has a white patch on the lower part of the back. The chin is white, but all the rest of the plumage, with the exception of the above-mentioned patch, is black or smoky brown.

This bird nests in colonies in the verandahs of houses and inside deserted buildings. The nest is a cup-shaped structure, usually built under an eave in the angle which a roof-beam makes with the wall. Thus the swift finds, ready-made, a roof and a couple of walls, and has merely to add the floor and remaining walls, in one of which it leaves a hole by way of entrance to the nursery. Thus the swift reverses the usual order of things, which is to erect a nest on some foundation such as a branch or ledge.

As we have seen, all four toes of the swift are for-wardly directed and each is terminated by a sharp hook-like claw. Thus the swift is able to cling with ease to such a vertical surface as that of a wall, and is therefore quite independent of any ledge or perch. The nest is a conglomeration of grass, straw, and feathers, which are made to adhere to one another, and to the building to which the nest is attached, by the cement-like saliva of the bird.

Some species of swift build their homes entirely of their glutinous saliva, and so manufacture "edible birds' nests." The Indian swift, however, utilises all manner of material by way of economising its saliva.

Nest building is a slow process. Each tiny piece of material has to be separately stuck on to the structure, and the saliva, which is, of course, liquid when first secreted, takes about five minutes to dry. During the whole of this time the bird remains motionless, holding *in situ* whatever it is adding to the structure.

I once timed a pair of swifts at work, and found that on an average they took forty-five minutes in bringing each new piece of material. Much of this time was undoubtedly spent in seeking for food, for so active a bird as the swift must have an enormous appetite, and, as it feeds on the minutest of insects, must consume thousands of them in the course of the day, each of which has to be caught separately. But, even allowing for this, the rate at which the material is added is very slow. Some naturalists declare that the swift is unable to pick anything off the ground. If this be so, the labour of obtaining material must be great, for the creature must fly about until it espies a feather or piece of straw floating in the air.

I am not yet in a position to say whether it is really impossible for the bird to pick anything from off the ground. I have never seen it do so, and it is a fact that the birds will, when building, eagerly seize anything floating in the air. On the other hand, the helplessness of the swift when placed upon the ground has been much exaggerated. It is said that the bird, if put upon

a flat surface, is unable to rise and will remain there
until it dies. Quite recently some Indian swifts were
brought to me and I placed one of them on my desk.
In less than twenty seconds the bird was flying about
in the room. Then, again, the grasping powers of its
hook-like claws have been somewhat magnified. The
bird in question made several unsuccessful attempts to
cling on to the whitewashed wall, and eventually fell
to the floor, where it was seized and then liberated in
the open. It flew off none the worse for its adventure.
Nevertheless, its claws are very sharp; the bird in
question stuck them quite unpleasantly into me when I
held it. A swift can certainly cling to any vertical
surface that is the least rough.

Unlike most birds, swifts use their nests as houses
and sleep in them at night. One frequently hears
issuing from the rafters in the dead of night the
piercing scream so characteristic of swifts. This
disposes of the silly story, so prevalent, that at evening
time the swifts mount into the higher layers of the
atmosphere and there sleep on the wing.

In conclusion, I must mention the characteristic
flight of swifts just before sundown. The birds close
the day in what has been called "a jubilant rout"; as
if they had not already taken sufficient exercise, they fly
at a breakneck pace round about the building in which
their nests are placed, dodging in and out of the pillars
of the verandah, and fill the air with their shivering
screams. This seems to be a characteristic of swifts
wherever they are found.

BIRDS AS AUTOMATA

THE sudden change that comes over the nature of most birds at the nesting season is, perhaps, the most wonderful phenomenon in nature. Active, restless birds, which normally spend the whole day on the wing, are content to sit motionless in a cramped position upon the nest for hours together. Birds of prey, whose nature it is to devour every helpless creature that comes within their grasp, behave most tenderly towards their young, actually disgorging swallowed food in order to provide them with a meal. Timid birds become bold. Those which under ordinary circumstances will not permit a human being to approach near them, will sometimes, while brooding, actually allow themselves to be lifted off the nest.

At the breeding season intelligence, which counsels self-preservation, gives way before the parental instinct, which causes birds to expose themselves to danger, and, in some cases, even to sacrifice their lives for the sake of their offspring.

From the construction of the nest until the time when the young ones are fledged the actions of the parent birds are, at any rate in the neighbourhood of the nest, those of automata, rather than of creatures endowed with intelligence.

On this hypothesis alone are many of the actions of nesting birds comprehensible.

That the construction of the nest is in the main an instinctive habit and not the result of intelligence is proved by the fact that a bird which has been hatched out in an incubator will, at the appointed season, build a nest.   If birds were not guided by instinct they would never take the trouble to do such a quixotic thing. What benefit can they derive from laboriously collecting a number of twigs and weaving them into a nest ?

It is, of course, natural selection that has originated this instinct ; for those species in which the parental instinct is not developed, or in which there is not some substitute for it, must inevitably perish.   When once this instinct has taken root natural selection will tend to perpetuate it, since those species which take the best care of their young are those which are likely to survive in the struggle for existence.

Many instances can be adduced to show how automatic are the actions of birds at the nesting season.

It sometimes happens that a bird lays an egg and then proceeds to build a nest on top of it.

Again, some birds do not know their own eggs. A whole clutch of different ones may be substituted for those upon which the bird is sitting and the bird will not discover the change.

The well-known bird-photographer, Mr. R. Kearton, was desirous of obtaining a good photograph of a sitting thrush, and as he was afraid that her eggs would be hatched before a fine, sunny day presented itself, had some wooden dummies made.   These he painted and varnished to look like those of the thrush, and put them in the nest, wondering whether the bird would be deceived. He need not have wondered; she would probably have sat upon the shams even had they not been coloured.

Upon another occasion Mr. Kearton replaced some starling nestlings by his wooden eggs, and waited to see what would happen. " In a few minutes," he writes, " back came the starling with a rush. She gazed in wonder at the contents of the nest for a few seconds, but, quickly making up her mind to accept the strangely altered condition of things, she sat down on the bits of painted wood without a trace of discontent in either look or action. Putting her off again, I reversed the order of things and waited. Upon returning, the starling stared in amazement at the change that had come over the scene during her absence; but her curiosity soon vanished, and she commenced to brood her chicks in the most matter-of-fact way." Then Mr. Kearton took out the chicks and put his fist into the nest, so that the back of his hand was uppermost. The starling actually brooded his knuckles. We must, of course, remember that a starling's nest is in a hole, where there is but little light. But, provided the starling could not see him, I believe that she would have brooded his knuckles in broad daylight.

Crows, the most intelligent of birds, will sit upon and try to hatch golf balls and ping-pong balls. One famous kite in Calcutta sat long and patiently in a vain attempt to make a pill-box yield a chick, while another member of this species subjected a hare's skull to similar treatment. Upon one occasion I took a robin's egg that was quite cold and placed it among the warm ones in a blackbird's nest. The hen came and brooded the egg along with her own without appearing to notice the addition, although it was much smaller than her eggs and of a totally different colour.

In the same way, if a set of nestlings of another species be substituted for those already in the nest, the parent birds will usually feed the new family without noticing the change. Instinct teaches a bird to brood all inanimate objects it sees in the nest and to feed all living things, whether they be its own offspring or not, and many birds blindly obey this instinct. It is, of course, to the advantage of the species that this should be so. For it is only on very rare occasions that foreign objects get into a nest, and nature cannot provide for such remote contingencies.

Similarly, instinct will not allow a bird to pay any attention to objects outside the nest, even though these objects be the bird's own offspring.

As everybody knows, the common cuckoo nestling ejects its foster-brethren from the nest, and if the true parents were able to appreciate what had happened, how much sorrow among its victims would the cuckoo cause! As a matter of fact, no sorrow at all is caused. Incredible as it may seem, the parent birds do not miss the young ones, nor do they appear to see them as they lie outside the nest. In this connection I cannot do better than quote Mr. W. H. Hudson, who was able to closely observe what happened when a young cuckoo had turned a baby robin out of the nest. " Here,"

writes Hudson, " the young robin when ejected fell a
distance of but five or six inches, and rested on a broad,
light green leaf, where it was an exceedingly conspicuous object; and when the mother robin was on
the nest—and at that stage she was on it the greater
part of the time—warming that black-skinned, toad-
like, spurious babe of hers, her bright, intelligent eyes
were looking full at the other one, just beneath her,
which she had grown in her body and had hatched with
her warmth, and was her very own.   I watched her for
hours ; watched her when warming the cuckoo, when
she left the nest, and when she returned with food and
warmed it again, and never once did she pay the least
attention to the outcast lying there close to her.   There
on its green leaf it remained, growing colder by degrees,
hour by hour, motionless, except when it lifted its head
as if to receive food, then dropped it again, and when at
intervals it twitched its body as if trying to move.
During the evening even these slight motions ceased,
though the feeblest flame of life was not yet extinct ;
but in the morning it was dead and cold and stiff ; and
just above it, her bright eyes upon it, the mother robin
sat on the nest as before warming the cuckoo."

Even those actions of nesting birds which appear to
be most intelligent can be shown to be merely automatic.
Take, for example, the curious habit of feigning injury,
which some birds have, when an enemy approaches the
young, in order to distract attention from them to itself
and thus enable them to seek cover unobserved.   This
surely seems a highly intelligent act.   But birds sometimes act thus before the eggs are hatched, and by so

doing actually attract attention to the eggs. This action is purely instinctive, and is perpetuated and strengthened by natural selection because it is beneficial to the race.

We have seen how at the nesting season all a bird's normal actions and instincts are subordinated to those of incubation. It is therefore but reasonable to suppose the incubating bird to be in a very peculiar and excitable state, a state bordering on insanity.

A bird in this condition might be expected to go into something resembling convulsions on the approach of an enemy, and, provided its acts under such circumstances tended to help the offspring to escape, and were at the same time not sufficiently acute to cause the mother bird to fall a victim to the enemy, natural selection would tend to perpetuate and fix such actions.

Want of space prevents further dilation upon this fascinating subject.

To sum up the conclusions I desire to emphasise. A bird has during the greater part of its life only to look after itself, and the more intelligent it be the better will it do this, hence natural selection tends to increase the intelligence of birds. But, at certain seasons, it becomes all-important to the species that the adults should attend to their young, even at risk to themselves. To secure this Nature has placed inside birds a force, dormant at most times, which at periodic intervals completely overrides all normal instincts, a force which compels parent birds to rivet their attention on the nest and its contents. Thus the sudden conversion of birds into automata is a necessity, not a mere whim of Dame Nature. The instinct is not of very long duration; for as soon as the

young are able to fend for themselves, the parents sometimes behave in what seems to human beings a most
unnatural way : they drive off their offspring by force.
As a matter of fact, this behaviour is quite natural; it
is dictated by Nature for the benefit of the species.
Strong as the maternal instinct is, it is liable to be over-
ridden by stronger instincts, such as that of migration.
When the time for the migratory journey comes round,
the parent birds will desert, without apparently a pang
of remorse, or even a thought, the broods for whose
welfare they have been slaving day and night. This
desertion of later broods by migratory birds is far
commoner than is generally supposed. In 1826 Mr.
Blackwell inspected the house-martins' nests under the
eaves of a barn at Blakely after the autumnal migration
of these birds. Of the twenty-two nests under the eaves
inspected on 11th November, no fewer than thirteen
were found to contain eggs and dead nestlings.

PLAYING CUCKOO

ORNITHOLOGICAL experience led me some time back to the belief that at the nesting season a bird becomes a creature of instinct, an organism whose actions are, for the time being, those of a machine, a mere automaton. This view, which has been set forth in the preceding article, is not held by all naturalists. I therefore determined to undertake a systematic series of experiments with a view to putting it to the test. In other words, I decided to play cuckoo. I selected the Indian crow (*Corvus splendens*) as the subject of my experiments, because it is the most intelligent of the feathered folk. If it can be proved that when on the nest the actions of this bird are mechanical, it will follow that the less intelligent birds are likewise mere automata when incubating. Another reason for selecting the crow as my victim is that I have been investigating the habits of the koel (*Eudynamis honorata*), which is parasitic on the crow, and in so doing have had to visit a large number of crows' nests.

The crow lays a pale blue egg blotched with brown, while the egg of the koel is a dull olive-green also blotched with brown. It is considerably smaller than the crow's egg. I have seen dozens of koel's eggs, but never one that

a human being could possibly mistake for that of a crow,
yet our friend *Corvus* is unable to detect the strange egg
when deposited in the nest and sits upon it.   It is not that
birds are colour-blind.   The koel is able to distinguish
its own egg from that of the crow, for, after it has
deposited its egg, it frequently returns to the nest and
removes one or more of the crow's eggs!   I am convinced that ordinarily a crow would have no difficulty in
distinguishing between the two kinds of egg; but at the
nesting time it throws most of its intelligence to the
winds and becomes a puppet in the hands of its instincts, which are to sit upon everything in the nest.

I have myself placed koel's eggs in crows' nests, and
in every case the crow has incubated the eggs.   On one
occasion I came upon a crow's nest containing only two
koel's eggs.   As the nest was some way from my bungalow and in an exposed situation, I knew that, the
moment I left, it would be robbed by some mischievous
native boy, so I took the eggs and placed them in a
crow's nest in my compound.   This already contained
three crow's eggs, two of which I moved, substituting
the koel's eggs for them.   The crow's eggs had only
been laid three or four days, but the koel's eggs were
nearly incubated, since both yielded chicks on the third
day after I placed them in the nest.   If nesting crows
think, that pair must have been somewhat surprised at
the speedy appearance of the chicks!

In all, I have placed six koel's eggs in four different
crow's nests, and as I have already said, in no single
instance did the trick appear to be detected.   In the
majority of cases, I did not trouble to keep the number

of eggs in the nest constant.   I merely added the koel's egg to those already in the nest.

But I have put my theory to a much more severe test. In a certain crow's nest containing two eggs I put a large fowl's egg. This was cream-coloured and fully three times the size of the crow's egg, yet within ten minutes the crow was sitting comfortably on the strange egg. She did not appear to notice the considerable addition to her clutch. She subsequently laid three more eggs, so that she had six eggs to sit upon, five of her own and the large fowl's egg! Day after day I visited the nest and watched the progress of the strange egg. On the twentieth day the chick inside was moving, but when I went to the nest on the twenty-first day I discovered that some one had climbed the tree, for several branches were broken. Two young crows had been taken away and the fowl's egg thrown upon the ground. There it lay with a fully formed black chicken inside! I have that chicken in a bottle of spirit. Subsequent inquiry showed that the *dhobi's* son had taken it upon himself to spoil my experiment. However, it went sufficiently far to prove that crows may one day become birds of economic value; why not employ them as incubators? Had the crow come across that chick's egg anywhere but in its nest, it would undoubtedly have made its breakfast off it.

I repeated the experiment in another nest. This time the chick hatched out. When it appeared the rage of the crows knew no bounds. With angry squawks the scandalised birds attacked the unfortunate chick, and so viciously did they peck at it that it was

I

in a dying state by the time my climber reached the nest.

With a view to determining at what stage the incubating instinct secures its dominance, I placed another fowl's egg in a crow's nest that was almost ready to receive eggs, wondering whether the presence of this egg would stimulate the crow to lay, without troubling to give the final touches to the nest. The bird devoured the egg. It is my belief that the acts of a nesting bird do not become completely automatic until it has laid an egg in the nest. If one visits a crow's nest which is in course of construction, the owners will as likely as not desert it; but I have never known a crow desert its nest when once it has laid an egg—provided, of course, he who visits the nest leaves any eggs in it.

In another nest containing two crow's eggs I placed a golf ball; on returning next day I found the crow sitting tight upon her own two eggs and the golf ball!

But in another case, where I had found two eggs and substituted for them a couple of golf balls, the crow refused to sit. I suppose the idea was, " I may be a bit of a fool when I am nesting, but I am not such a fool as all that!" I once came across a young koel and a crow's egg in a nest. I removed the former and placed it in a crow's nest containing four crow's eggs. The owner of the nest showed no surprise at the sudden appearance of the koel, but set about feeding it in the most matter-of-fact way. The young koel was successfully reared; it is now at large and will next year victimise some crow. I may say that no human being could possibly fail to distinguish between a young koel and a young

THE INDIAN PADDY BIRD. (ARDEOLA GRAYII)

crow. When first hatched the koel has a black skin, the crow a pink one. The mouth of the crow nestling is an enormous triangle with great fleshy flaps at the side; the mouth of the koel is much smaller and lacks the flaps. The feathers arise very differently in each species, and whereas those of the crow are black, those of the koel are tipped with russet in the cock and white in the hen.

In another nest containing a young koel (put there by me) and two crow's eggs, I placed a paddy bird's (*Ardeola grayii*) egg, hoping that the gallant crow would hatch it out and appreciate the many-sidedness of her family. She hatched out the egg all right, at least I believe she did. I saw it in the nest the day before the young paddy bird was due; but when I visited the nest the following morning neither egg nor young bird was there. It would seem that the crow did not appreciate the appearance of the latest addition to the family and destroyed it. It is, of course, possible that the young koel declined to associate with such a neighbour and killed it; but I think that the crow was the culprit, for I had previously placed a paddy bird nestling, four days old, in a crow's nest containing only young crows, and the paddy bird had similarly disappeared.

These, then, are the main facts which my game of cuckoo has brought to light. They are not so decisive as I had expected. They seem to indicate that the actions of birds with eggs or young are not quite so mechanical as I had supposed. Were they not largely mechanical a crow would never hatch out a koel's egg, nor would it feed the young koel when hatched out; it would not incubate a fowl's or a paddy bird's egg, and it would assuredly decline to sit upon a golf ball. On the other hand, were the acts of nesting birds altogether mechanical, the young paddy birds would have been reared up, and the substitution of two golf balls for two eggs would not have been detected. There is apparently a limit to the extent to which intelligence is subservient to blind instinct.

THE KOEL

NGLO-INDIANS frequently confound the koel with the brain-fever bird. There is certainly some excuse for the mistake, for both are cuckoos and both exceedingly noisy creatures ; but the cry of the koel (*Eudynamis honorata*) bears to that of the brain-fever bird or hawk-cuckoo (*Hierococcyx varius*) much the same relation as the melody of the organ-grinder does to that of a full German band. Most men are willing to offer either the solitary Italian or the Teutonic gang a penny to go into the next street, but, if forced to choose between them, select the organ-grinder as the lesser of the two evils. In the same way, most people find the fluty note of the koel less obnoxious than the shriek of the hawk-cuckoo.

The latter utters a treble note, which sounds like "Brain fever." This it is never tired of repeating. It commences low down the musical scale and then ascends higher and higher until you think the bird must burst. But it never does burst. When the top note is reached the exercise is repeated.

The koel is a bird of many cries. As it does not, like the brain-fever bird, talk English, its notes are not easy to reproduce on paper. Its commonest call is a crescendo *kuil, kuil, kuil,* from which the bird derives its

popular name.   This cry is peculiar to the cock.   The
second note is, to use the words of Colonel Cunningham,
" an outrageous torrent of shouts, sounding like *kūk, kŭū,
kŭū, kŭū, kŭū, kŭū*, repeated at brief intervals in tones
loud enough to rouse the ' Seven Sleepers.' "   The koel
is nothing if not impressive.   He likes to utter this note
just before dawn, when all the world is still.   As the
bird calls chiefly in the hot weather, when it frequently
happens that the hour before sunrise is almost the only
one in the twenty-four in which the jaded European can
sleep, this note is productive of much evil language on
the part of the aforesaid European.

The koel's third cry is well described by Cunningham
as a mere cataract of shrill shrieks—*heekaree, karees*.
This is heard mostly when the hen is fleeing for dear
life before a pair of outraged crows.   So much for the
voice of the koel, now for a description of the singer.
The cock is a jet-black bird with a green bill and a red
eye.   The hen is speckled black and white, with the eye
and beak as in the cock.   Add to this the fact that the
koel is a little larger than the " merry cuckoo, messenger
of spring " which visits England, and it is impossible not
to recognise the bird.

This cuckoo, like many of its relatives, does not hatch
its own eggs.   It cuckolds crows.   This is no mean
performance, for the crow is a suspicious creature.   It
knoweth full well the evil which is in its own heart, and
so, judging others by itself, watches unceasingly over its
nest from the time the first egg is deposited therein
until the hour when the most backward young one is
able to fly.   Now, a koel is no match for a crow in open

fight, hence it is quite useless for the former to attempt by means of force to introduce its egg into the crow's nest. It is obliged to resort to guile. The cock entices away the crows, and while they are absent the hen deposits her egg.

Crows appear to dislike the cry of the koel quite as much as men do. But whereas man is usually content with swearing at the noisy cuckoo, crows attack it with beak and claw whenever an opportunity offers. This fact is turned to account by the koel. The cock alights in a tree near a crow's nest and begins to call. The owners of the nest, sooner or later, "go for" him. He then takes to his wings, continuing to call, so as to induce the crows to prolong the chase. As he is a more rapid flier than they, he does not run much risk. While the irate corvi are in pursuit, the hen koel, who has been lurking around, slips into the nest and there lays her egg. If she is given time she destroys one or more of those already in the nest. She does this, not because the crows would detect the presence of an additional egg, but in order that her young, when hatched, will not be starved owing to the large number of mouths to feed.

Crows, although such clever birds, are, as we have seen, remarkably stupid at the nesting season. They are unable to distinguish the koel's egg from their own, although the former is considerably smaller, with an olive-green background instead of a bluish one; and when the young koel emerges from the egg, they are unable to differentiate between it and their own off-spring, although baby koels are black and baby crows pink, when first hatched out. The koel nestling has one point in common with young crows, and that is a large mouth of which the inside is red. This is opened wide whenever a parent approaches, so that the latter sees nothing but a number of yawning caverns; thus there is some excuse for its failure to distinguish between the true and the spurious nestlings.

To return to the koel who is laying her egg in the momentarily deserted nest. She does not carry her egg thither in her beak as the common cuckoo is said to do, but sits in the nest and lays it there. Sometimes the crows return before she is ready and, of course, attack her, but as she can fly faster than they, they do not often succeed in harming her, although there are instances on record of crows mobbing female koels to death. It will thus be seen that cuckolding crows is dangerous work. The life of the cuckoo is not all beer and skittles, and the birds seem to feel the danger of their existence, for at the breeding season they appear to be in a most excited state, and are manifestly afraid of the crows. This being so, I am inclined to think that the latter are responsible for the parasitic habit of the koel. It is not improbably a case of the biter bit. Crows are such aggressive birds that they are quite capable of evicting any other bird from its nest if this be large enough to suit their purpose. Now suppose a koel to be thus evicted by force when ready to lay; it is quite conceivable that she might make frantic efforts to lay in her rightful nest, and if she succeeded, and the crows failed to detect her egg, they would hatch out her offspring. If the koels which acted thus managed to have their offspring reared for them, while those that attempted to build fresh nests dropped their eggs before the new nurseries were ready, natural selection would tend to weed out the latter and thus the parasitic habit might arise, until eventually the koel came to forget how to build a nest.

In this connection it is important to bear in mind that the nearest relatives of the koel are non-parasitic. It is therefore not improbable that in the koel the parasitic habit has an independent origin.

This instinct has undoubtedly been evolved more than once. It does not necessarily follow that similar causes have led to its origin in each case.

The suggestion I have made is made only with reference to the koel, which differs from other cuckoos in that it dupes a bird stronger and bigger than itself. But this is a digression.

If the koel have time, she destroys one or more of the existing eggs, and will sometimes return later and destroy others. Although the crow cannot distinguish between her own and koel's eggs, the koel can. I have come across several crows' nests which each contained only two koel's eggs.

The young koel is a better-behaved bird than some of its relations, for it ejects neither the eggs still in the nest when it is hatched nor its foster-brethren. But the incubating period of the koel is shorter than that of the crow, so that the koel's egg is always the first to hatch out. The koel seems never to make the mistake of depositing its egg among nearly incubated ones. Thus the young koel commences life with a useful start on its foster-brethren. It soon increases this start, as it grows very fast, and is ready to fly before the earliest feathers of its foster-brothers are out of their sheaths.

It does not, however, leave its foster-parents when able to fly. It sits on the edge of the nest and makes laudable, if ludicrous, efforts at cawing. The crows continue feeding it long after it has left the nest, looking after it with the utmost solicitude. A young koel is somewhat lacking in intelligence; it seems unable to distinguish its foster-parents from any other crow, for it opens its mouth at the approach of every crow, evidently expecting to be fed.

The natives of the Punjab assert that the hen koel keeps her eye on the crow's nest in which she has laid her egg or eggs during the whole of the time that the young cuckoo is in it, and takes charge of her babe after it leaves the nest. This assertion appears to be incorrect. I have never seen a koel feeding anything but itself. Moreover, the koel lays four or five eggs, and these are not usually all deposited in one nest. It would therefore be exceedingly difficult, if not impossible, for the hen to keep an eye on each of her eggs.

In view of the hatred which crows display towards koels in general, naturalists have expressed surprise that the young koels are not mobbed directly they leave the nest. Their plumage differs in no way from that of the adult. It has been suggested that young koels retain the crow smell for a considerable time after they are fledged. This I cannot accept. The olfactory organ of birds is but slightly developed. Indeed, I am inclined to wonder whether birds have any sense of smell. The truth of the matter is that crows look after their foster-children most carefully for several weeks after they have left the nest, and see that no strange crow harms them.

THE COMMON DOVES OF INDIA

THE dove family ought to have become extinct ages ago, if all that orthodox zoologists tell us about the fierce struggle for existence be true. They form a regular "Thirteen Society." They do everything they should not do, they disobey every rule of animal warfare, they fall asleep when sitting exposed on a telegraph wire, they build nests in all manner of foolish places, their nests are about as unsafe as a nursery can possibly be, and they flatly decline to lay protectively coloured eggs—their white eggs are a standing invitation to bird robbers to indulge, like the Cambridge crew of 1906, in an egg diet; yet, in spite all of these foolhardy acts, doves flourish like the green bay tree. This is a fact of which I require an explanation before I can accept all the doctrines of the Neo-Darwinian school.

There are so many species of dove in India that when speaking of them one must perforce, unless one be writing a great monograph, confine oneself to two or three of the common species. I propose to-day to talk about our three commonest Indian doves, that is to say, the spotted dove (*Turtur suratensis*), the Indian ring-dove (*Turtur risorius*), and the little brown dove (*Turtur cambayensis*). I make no apology for discoursing upon these common species. I contend that we in India know so very little about even our everyday birds that it is a needless expenditure of energy to seek out the rarer species and study their habits; we have plenty to learn about those that come into our verandahs and coo to us.

The curious distribution of our common Indian doves has not, so far as I know, been explained. In very few places are all three common. One or other of them is usually far more abundant than the others, and this one is usually the spotted dove. It is the commonest dove of Calcutta, of Madras, of Travancore, of Tirhoot, of Lucknow, but not of Lahore or Bombay or the Deccan. Why is this? Why is it that, whereas the Deccan is literally overrun by the ring- and the little brown dove, one can go from Bombay to Malabar without meeting one of these species, but seeing thousands of the spotted dove?

The only explanation that I can offer of this phenomenon is that the spotted dove is the most pugnacious and the most pushing; that where he chooses to settle down he ousts the other species of dove more or less completely; but he, fortunately for the other species, does not choose to settle down in all parts of India. He objects to dry places. Hence he is not seen at Lahore or in the Deccan, or in the drier parts of the United Provinces, such as Agra, Muttra, Etawah, and Cawnpore.

This is only a theory of mine, and a theory in favour of which I am not able to adduce very much evidence, since my personal knowledge of India is confined to some half-a-dozen widely separated places. Moreover, this theory does not explain the absence of the spotted dove from Bombay. I should be very glad to know if there are any other moist parts of India where the spotted dove is not the most abundant of the cooing family.

The nest of the dove is a subject over which most ornithologists have waxed sarcastic. A more ramshackle structure does not exist; yet the absurd thing is that doves are most particular about the materials they use.

The other day I watched, with much amusement, a little brown dove at work nest building. It was constructing a shake-down in a small Lonicera bush. Now, obviously, since the nest is just a few twigs and stalks thrown together, any kind of short twig or stem will serve for building material. This, however, was not the view of the dove. If that creature had been constructing the Forth Bridge it could not have been more particular as regards the materials it picked up. It strutted about the ground, taking into its bill all manner of material only to reject it, until at last it picked up a dead grass stalk and flew off with it in triumph!

Presumably doves take the same trouble in selecting a site for their nest, nevertheless they sometimes eventually choose the most impossible spot. Thus Mr. A. Anderson has recorded the existence of a nest of a pair of little brown doves that " was placed close to the fringe of the *kunnaut* of his tent on one of the corner ropes, where it is double for some six inches and there knotted.   The double portion was just broad enough, being three inches apart, to support the nest with careful balancing; the *knot* acted as a sort of *buffer* and prevented the twigs from sliding off, which most assuredly would otherwise have been the case, for the rope just there was at an angle of 45°."

Those foolish birds were not permitted to bring up their young, because the tent had to be struck before the eggs were laid.

In Lahore a favourite nesting site for the little brown dove is on the top of the rolled-up portion of the verandah *chik*. As the *chik* is composed of stout material, the rolled-up portion forms an excellent platform some four inches broad.   But as the doves nest just as the weather is beginning to grow warm, the little home is apt to be somewhat rudely broken up. One pair, however, has this year successfully reared up two young hopefuls in a nest on this somewhat precarious site.   The doings of these form the subject of the next article.

I once came across a nest of this little dove in a low, prickly bush beside a small canal distributory, three miles outside Lahore. The dove appeared to have used as the foundation for its nest an old one of the striated bush babbler (*Argya caudata*).   (I object to calling this bird the common babbler, since, like common sense, it is not very common.)   In the same bush, at the same level, that is to say, about a yard from the ground and only a couple of feet from the dove's nest, was that of a striated bush babbler containing three dark blue eggs. This is a case upon which those who believe that eggs laid in open nests are protectively coloured would do well to ponder.

There, side by side, in precisely the same environment, were two nests—one containing white and the other dark blue eggs. Obviously both sets of eggs could not be protectively coloured ; as a matter of fact, both clutches of eggs were conspicuous objects. It not infrequently happens that the Indian robin (*Thamnobia cambayensis*), which lays white eggs thickly spotted with reddish brown, brings up a family in a disused nest of a striated bush babbler's. The eggs of this latter are dark blue. It is surely time that zoologists gave up throwing at us their everlasting theory of protective colouring. If this were a *sine qua non* of the safety of birds' eggs, then the whole dove tribe would, long ago, have ceased to exist.

This family presents the ornithologist with yet another problem in colouration. In every species, except the red turtle-dove (*Oenopopelia tranquebarica*), both sexes are coloured alike. In this latter, however, there is very pronounced sexual dimorphism. The ruddy wing feathers of the cock enable one to distinguish him at once from his mate and from every other dove. Now the habits of this dove appear to be exactly like those of all other species. It constructs the same kind of nest and in similar situations ; why then the sexual dimorphism in this species and in no other species? If the lady rufous turtle-dove likes nice ruddy wings, and thus the red wing has been evolved in the cock bird, why has she too not inherited it? I presume that even the most audacious Neo-Darwinian will not talk about her greater need of protection when sitting on the nest, for if she needs protection, how much more so do her white eggs? Further, it is my belief that the cock bird takes his turn in the incubation.

It must not be thought that I am needlessly poking fun at modern biologists. I merely desire to call attention to the unsolved problems that confront us on all sides, and to protest against the dogmatism of biology which declares that the Darwinian theory explains the whole of organic nature. As a matter of fact, it seems to me that the field naturalist cannot but feel that natural selection is turning out rather a failure.

In conclusion, one more word regarding the red turtle-dove. Its distribution has not been carefully worked out, and what we do know of it is not easy to explain. Hume says that it breeds in all parts of India, but is very capriciously distributed, and he is unable to say what kind of country it prefers, and why it is common in one district and rare in a neighbouring one in which all physical conditions appear identical.

It is very common in the bare, arid, treeless region that surrounds the Sambhur Lake. It is common in some dry, well-cultivated districts, like Etawah, where there are plenty of old mango groves. It is very common in some of the comparatively humid tracts, like Bareilly, and again in the *sal* jungles of the Kumaun *Bhabar* and the Nepal *Terai*. On the other hand, over wide extents of similar country it is scarcely to be seen. Doubtless there is something in its food or manner of life that limits its distribution, but no one has yet been able to make out what this something is.

K

DOVES IN A VERANDAH

THE office building in which for some time past I have rendered service to a paternal government was once a tomb. That it is now an office is evidence of the strict economy practised by the Indian Administration. Since the living require more light than the dead, skylights have been let into the domed roof. In these the brown rock-chat (*Cercomela fusca*) loves to sit and pour forth his exceedingly sweet little lay, while his spouse sits on four pale blue eggs in a nest on a ledge in a neighbouring sepulchre. But it is not of this bird that I write to-day; I hope to give him an innings at some future date.

Two little brown doves (*Turtur cambaiensis*) first demand our attention, since these for a time appropriated my skylights. This species is smaller than the spotted dove so common in Madras, and, to my way of thinking, is a much more beautiful bird. Its head, neck, and breast are pale lilac washed with red. On each side of the neck the bird carries a miniature chess-board. The remainder of its plumage is brown, passing into grey and white. The legs are lake-red.

It has a very distinctive note—a soft, subdued musical *cuk-cuk-coo-coo-coo*. There is no bird better pleased with itself than the little brown dove. In the month of March the two doves in question were " carrying on " in my office skylight to such an extent as to leave no doubt that they had a nest somewhere. I discovered it on the rolled-up end of one of the bamboo verandah *chiks*. These are not let down in the cold weather, so that the doves had been permitted to build undisturbed.

" Eha " has humorously described a dove's nest as composed of two short sticks and a long one ; that of the little brown dove is a little more compact than the typical nest, a little less sketchy, and composed of grass and fine twigs. There was plenty of room for it on the top of the rolled-up portion of the *chik*.

When I found the nest there were two white eggs in it. Every species of dove lays but two eggs. I do not know whether the smallness of the clutch has anything to do with the helplessness of the young birds when first hatched. Young doves and pigeons have not, like other baby birds, great mouths which open to an alarming extent. They feed by putting their beaks in the mouth of the parent and there they obtain " pigeon's milk," which is a secretion from the crop of the old birds.

Being at that time less versed in the ways of the little brown dove than I now am, I was under the impression that this nest was in rather a curious situation, so I determined to obtain a photograph of it with the young birds. I may here say that I dislike photography, and not without cause. Some years ago I visited the Himalayan snows, and dragged up a great camera and a number of plates to an altitude of 12,000 feet. Having no portable dark room, I endured untold agonies while changing the plates under the bedclothes. Being anxious lest the light should reach the exposed negatives, I wrapped them up very carefully, using newspaper, which was the only wrapping available. When I returned from the expedition I developed the plates, but lo and behold! instead of snowy peaks and sunny valleys, advertisements of soaps and pills appeared on the plates. Why do not books on the camera tell one not to wrap up plates in newspaper? I made a vow to leave photography to others, and I kept the vow until I saw those young doves perched so temptingly on the *chik*.

Having risked both life and limb in mounting a chair placed upon a table, I obtained a "snap" at the nest. On developing the plate everything appeared with admirable clearness except the nest. There was nothing but a blur where this should have been ; the rest of the *chik* came out splendidly. The only explanation of this phenomenon that I can offer is the natural "cussedness" of the camera. I have now renewed my vow to eschew photography.

The first young doves were successfully reared. No sooner had they been driven forth into the world than the parents set about repairing the nest, for doves are not content with one brood; when once a pair commence nesting there is no knowing when they will stop. As it was then April and the sun was growing uncomfortably hot, the letting down of the *chik* became a matter of necessity, and this, of course, wrecked the nest. I expected to see no more of the doves. In this I was mistaken. Before long they were billing and cooing as merrily as before. A little search showed that this time they had built a nest on the top of the same *chik*—a feat which I should have thought impossible had I not seen the nest with my own eyes. Some sacking was attached to the *chik*, and this, together with the bamboo, presented a surface of about half an inch. On this precarious foundation the nest rested ; the twigs, of course, reached over to the wall from which the *chik* was hung. Thus the nest received some additional support. Needless to say, the young birds had to remain very still or they would have fallen out of the nest.

The second and the third broods were raised without mishap. One of the birds of the fourth family was more restless than his brethren had been ; consequently he fell off the nest on to the floor of the verandah. He was picked up and brought to me. Although not strong enough to walk, or even stand, he showed unmistakable signs of that evil temper which characterises all doves, by opening his wings and pecking savagely at my hand. In spite of this behaviour I set natural selection at naught by putting him back into the nest. He fell out again next day and was again replaced. This time he stayed there, and is now probably at large.

When the fifth clutch of eggs was in the nest my *chaprassi*, who, since I have shown him how to play cuckoo, has been upsetting the domestic affairs of any number of birds, asked whether he might substitute two pigeon's eggs for those laid by the dove. The substitution was duly effected without rousing any suspicions on the part of the doves. The young pigeons soon hatched out and were industriously fed by their foster-parents, nor did these latter appear to notice anything unusual when the white plumage of the pigeons appeared. Two days before the changelings were ready to fly a terrific storm arose and so shook the *chiks* that the poor pigeons were thrown off and killed. Nothing daunted, the doves have since successfully reared a sixth family! Can we wonder that doves are numerous in India?

THE GOLDEN ORIOLE

DAME Nature must have been in a very generous mood when she manufactured golden orioles, or she would never have expended so much of her colour-box upon them. Orioles are birds which compel our attention, so brilliant are they; yet the poets who profess to be the high-priests of Nature give us no songs about these beautiful creatures; at least I know of no maker of verse, with the exception of Sir Edwin Arnold, who does more than mention the oriole. Here then is a fine opening for some twentieth-century bard!

Two orioles, or mango birds as they are sometimes called, are common in India. They are the Indian oriole (*Oriolus kundoo*) and the black-headed oriole (*O. melanocephalus*). The Indian oriole is a bird about the size of a starling. The plumage of the cock is a splendid rich yellow. There is a black patch over and behind the eye. There is some black on the tail, and the large wing feathers are also of this colour. The bill is pink and the eyes red. In the hen the yellow of the back is deeply tinged with green.

The black-headed oriole may be distinguished by his black head, throat, and upper breast. The habits of both species are similar in every respect. The

Indian oriole seems to be merely a winter visitor to Madras, and it is seen in the Punjab only during the hot weather. In the intervening parts it may be observed all the year round; hence the species would appear to perform a small annual migration, leaving the South in the hot weather. In those parts where orioles are found all the year round it is not improbable that the birds one sees in the winter are not those that are observed during the summer.

The oriole is essentially a bird of the greenwood tree; if you would see him you should betake yourself to some well-irrigated orchard. I have never seen an oriole on the ground; its habits are strictly arboreal, but it does not seem to be at all particular about taking cover. It perches by preference on the topmost bough of a tree, and if this bough be devoid of leaves, so much the better, for the bird enjoys a more extensive view of the surrounding country. Very beautiful does such a bird look, sitting outlined against the sky, as the first rays of the morning sun fall upon and add fresh lustre to its golden plumage. Orioles feed upon both fruit and insects, and so cannot be regarded as unmixed blessings to the agriculturalist.

As I have already said, Dame Nature has been exceedingly kind to this bird; not content with decking him out in brilliantly coloured raiment, she has endowed him with a voice of which any bird might well be proud. It is a clear, mellow whistle, which is usually syllabised as *peeho, peeho,* or *lorio, lorio;* indeed, the name oriole is probably onomatopoetic. In addition to this the bird has several other notes.

These are not pleasant to the ear and may be described as blends, in varying proportions, of the harsh call of the king-crow and the *miau* of a cat. The hen almost invariably utters such a note when a human being approaches the nest; but the cry apparently does not always denote alarm, for I have heard an oriole uttering it when sitting placidly in a tree, seemingly at peace with all the world; but perhaps that particular bird may have been indulging in unpleasant day dreams; who knows?

We hear much of the marvellous nests of tailor- and weaver-birds, but never of that of the oriole. Naturalists, equally with poets, have neglected this beautiful species. An oriole's nest is in its way quite as wonderful as that of the tailor-bird. If a man were ordered to erect a cradle up in a tree, he would, I imagine, construct it precisely as the oriole does its nest. This last is a cup-shaped structure slung on to two or three branches of a tree by means of fibres which are wound first round one branch, then passed under the nest, and finally wound round another bough. The nest is therefore, as Hume pointed out, secured to its supporting branches in much the same way as a prawn net is to its wooden framework.

In places where there are mulberry trees the oriole shaves off narrow strips of the thin, pliable bark and uses these to support the nest. Jerdon describes one wonderful nest, taken by him at Saugor, that was suspended by a long roll of cloth about three-quarters of an inch wide, which the bird must have pilfered from some neighbouring verandah. "This strip," he states, "was wound round each limb of the fork, then passed round the nest beneath, fixed to the other limb, and again brought round the nest to the opposite side ; there were four or five of these supports on either side." The nest was so securely fixed that it could not have been removed till the supporting bands had been cut or had rotted away. Here then is an example of workmanship which the modern jerry-builder might well emulate.

I have made repeated attempts to see orioles at work on the supports of the nest, but so far have only managed to observe them lining it. Upon one occasion I came upon a nest some fifteen feet from the ground from which hung two strips of fibre about sixteen inches long that had been wound round one branch. I waited for some time, hoping the birds would return and allow me to see them finish the adjustment of these fibres ; but unfortunately there was no cover available, and the oriole is an exceedingly shy bird ; it will not do anything to the nest if it knows it is being watched.

The completed nursery, viewed from below, looks like a ball of dried grass wedged into the fork of a branch, and may easily be mistaken for that of a king-crow, but this last is, of course, not bound to the branches like that of the oriole.

A very curious thing that I have noticed about the Indian oriole's nest is that it is always situated either in the same tree as a king-crow's nest or in an adjacent tree. I have seen some thirteen or fourteen orioles' nests since I first noticed this phenomenon, and have, in every case, found a king-crow's nest within ten yards.

The drongo builds earlier, for it is usually feeding its young while the oriole is incubating. It would therefore appear that it is the oriole which elects to build near the king-crow. I imagine that it does so for the sake of protection; it must be a great thing for a timid bird to have a vigorous policeman all to itself, a policeman who will not allow a big creature to approach under any pretext whatever.

The oriole lays from two to four white eggs spotted with reddish brown. These spots readily wash off, and sometimes the colour "runs" and gives the whole egg a pink hue. Although both sexes take part in the construction of the nursery, the work of incubation appears to fall entirely upon the hen. I have never seen a cock oriole sitting on the nest.

THE BARN OWL

THE barn owl is a cosmopolitan bird. It is an adaptive species, and so has been able to make itself at home all the world over. Like every widely distributed species, including man, it has its local peculiarities. The barn owls of India are somewhat different from those of Africa, and these latter, again, may be readily distinguished from those that dwell in Europe. This any one may see for himself by paying a visit to the Zoological Gardens at Regent's Park, where barn owls from all parts of the world blink out their lives in neighbouring cages. Needless to say, species-mongers have tried to magnify these local peculiarities into specific differences. The European bird is known as *Strix flammea*. An attempt was made to differentiate the Indian barn owl. If you look up the bird in Jerdon's classical work you will see that it is called *Strix javanica*. Jerdon's justification for making a new species of it was its larger size, more robust feet and toes, and the presence of spots on the lower plumage. If such were specific differences we ought to divide up man, *Homo sapiens*, into quite a large number of species: *Homo major*, *H. minor*, *H. longirostris*, *H. brevirostris*, etc.

However, neither with the barn owl nor with man has the species-maker had his own way. Ornithologists recognise but one barn owl. This bird, which is frequently called the screech owl, is delightfully easy to describe. Everybody knows an owl when he sees one; but stay, I forgot the German Professor, mentioned by Mr. Bosworth Smith, who held up in triumph the owl which he had shot, saying: "Zee, I have shot von schnipe mit einem face Push cat." Let me therefore say it is easy enough for the average man to recognise an owl, but it is quite another matter when it comes to "spotting" the species to which an individual happens to belong. As a rule the family likeness is so strong as to overshadow specific differences. The barn owl, however, differs from all others in that it has a long, thin face. Take any common or garden owl, and you will observe that it has a round, plum-pudding-like head. Place that owl before one of those mirrors which make everything look long and thin, and you will see in the glass a very fair representation of the barn owl. The face of this owl, when it is awake, is heart-shaped; when the bird is asleep it is as long as that of a junior Madras Civil Servant as he looks over the Civil List. Whether awake or asleep, the bird has an uncanny, half-human look. It is innocent of the "ears" or "horns" which form so conspicuous a feature of some owls. In passing, I may say that those horn-like tufts of feathers have no connection with the well-developed auditory organ of the owl.

The barn owl's face is white, as is its lower plumage, hence it is popularly known in England as the white owl. The back and upper plumage are pale grey. The tail is buff, and there is a good deal of buff scattered about the rest of the plumage; it is on this account that the bird is called *flammea*.

The barn owl is, I believe, common in all parts of India, but it is not often seen owing to its strictly nocturnal habits. It ventures not forth into the dazzling light of day as does that noisy little clown, the spotted owlet (*Athene brama*). Should it happen to be abroad in daylight the crows make its life a burden. Friend Corvus is a very conservative individual. He sets his face steadfastly against any addition to the local fauna. As he seldom or never sees the barn owl, he does not include it among the birds of his locality; so that when one does show its face, the crows proceed to mob it. Their efforts are well seconded by the small fry among birds, who seem instinctively to dislike the whole owl tribe.

During the day the barn owl sleeps placidly in the interior of a decayed tree, or in a tomb, mosque, temple, or ruin, or even in the secluded verandah of a bungalow. The last place of abode is unsatisfactory from the point of view of the owl, for Indian servants display an antipathy towards it quite as great as that shown by the crows. They believe that the owls bring bad luck, and are in this respect not one whit more foolish than ignorant folk in other parts of the world. This useful and amusing bird is everywhere regarded with superstitious dread by the uneducated.

It lives almost exclusively on rats, mice, shrews, and other enemies of the farmer. And as an exceptional case it will take a young bird, which is usually a sparrow. Most people will agree that we can spare a few sparrows; nevertheless, that cruel idiot, the game-keeper, classes the barn owl as vermin and shoots it whenever he has the chance. This is fairly often, owing to the confiding habits of the creature. It will enter a bungalow after rats or moths, and will sometimes terrify the timid sleeper by sitting on the end of his bed and screaming at him!

The owl is blessed with an appetite that would do credit to an alderman. Lord Lilford states that he saw "a young half-grown barn owl take down nine full-grown mice, one after another, until the tail of the ninth stuck óut of his mouth, and in three hours' time was crying for more." Let me anticipate the captious critic by saying that it was the owl and not the tail of the ninth mouse that, like Oliver Twist, called for more. Moreover, the tail did not, as might be supposed, stick out because the bird was "full up inside." The barn owl invariably swallows a mouse head first; it makes a mighty gulp, with the result that the whole of the mouse, except the tail, disappears. Thus the victim remains for a short time in order that the owl may enjoy the *bonne bouche*. Then the tail disappears suddenly, and the curtain is rung down on the first act of the tragedy. The second and third acts are like unto the first. The last act is not very polite, but it must be described in the interests of science. After an interval of a few hours the owl throws up, in the form of a pellet, the bones, fur, and other undigestible portions of his victims. This is, of course, very bad manners, but it is the inevit-

able result of bolting a victim whole.   One vice, alas!
leads to another.

Kingfishers, which swallow whole fish, likewise eject
the bones.   This habit of the owl has enabled zoologists
to disprove the contention of the gamekeeper that the
barn owl lives chiefly upon young pheasants.   The
bones found in these pellets are nearly all those of
small rodents.

The screech owl, as its name implies, is not a great
songster.   It hisses, snores, and utters, during flight,
blood-curdling screams, which doubtless account for
its evil reputation.   It lays roundish white eggs in a
hole in a tree or other convenient cavity.   Three, four,
or six are laid, according to taste.   I have never found
the eggs in India, but they are, in England at any rate,
laid, not in rapid succession, but at considerable intervals,
so that one may find, side by side in a nest, eggs and
young birds of various ages.   I do not know whether
the owl derives any benefit from this curious habit.
It has been suggested that the wily creature makes the
first nestling which hatches out do some of the incubating.   Pranks of this kind are all very well when the
nest is hidden away in a hole; they would not do in
an open nest to which crows and other birds of that
feather have access.

A TREE-TOP TRAGEDY

IF I were a bird I would give the Indian crow a very wide berth, and, whenever I did come into unavoidable contact with him, I should behave towards him with the most marked civility. A clannishness prevails among crows which makes them nasty enemies to tackle. If you insult one of the "treble-dated" birds you find that the whole of the *corvi* of the neighbourhood resent that insult as if it had been addressed to each and every one individually, and if you get back nothing more than your insult *plus* very liberal interest, you are indeed lucky. In the same way, crows will revenge an injury tenfold. The eye-for-an-eye doctrine does not satisfy them; for an eye they want at least a pair of eyes, to say nothing of a complete set of teeth. I recently witnessed an example of what crows are capable of doing by way of revenge.

A couple of kites built high up in a lofty tree the clumsy platform of sticks which we dignify by the name "nest." This was furnished, soon after its completion, by a clutch of three straw-coloured eggs, handsomely blotched with red.

The uglist birds seem to lay the most beautiful eggs; this is perhaps the compensation which Dame Nature gives them for their own lack of comeliness.

The kite is a very close sitter. Like the crow, she knoweth the wickedness of her own heart, and as she judges others by herself, deems it necessary to continually mount guard over her eggs. Patience eventually meets with its reward. Three weeks of steady sitting result in the appearance of the young kites.

This long and patient sitting on the part of parent birds is, when one comes to think of it, a most remarkable phenomenon. No sooner do the eggs appear in the nest than the most active little bird seems to lose all its activity and become quite sedentary in its habits. Take, for example, the sprightly white-browed fantail flycatcher (*Rhipidura albifrontata*), a bird which ordinarily seems to have St. Vitus's dance in every organ and appendage. This species will, when it has eggs, sit as closely or more closely than a barndoor hen, and will sometimes allow you to stroke it. I often wonder what are the feelings of such a bird when incubating. One is tempted to think that it must find the process intensely boring. But this cannot be so, or it would refuse to sit. The fowls of the air are not hampered by the Ten Commandments; they are free to do that to which the spirit moveth them, without let or hindrance, without fear of arrest or prosecution for breach of the law. Hence birds must positively enjoy sitting on their eggs. At the brooding season avine nature undergoes a complete change. Ordinarily a bird delights to expend its ebullient energy in vigorous motion, just as a strong man delights to run a race; but at the nesting season its inclinations change; then its greatest joy is to sit upon its nest. Even as human beings are suddenly

THE COMMON KINGFISHER. (ALCEDO ISPIDA)
(One of the British birds found in India)

seized with the Bridge craze and are then perfectly content to sit for hours at the card table, so at certain seasons are birds overcome by the incubating mania. If my view of the matter be correct, and I think it must be, a sitting bird is no more an object for our pity than is a Bridge maniac. But this is a digression.

Let us hie back to our kite and her family of young ones in their lofty nursery. For a time all went well with them. But one day the sun of prosperity which had hitherto shone upon them became darkened by great black clouds of adversity. I happened to pass the nest at this time and saw about twenty excited crows squatting on branches near the nest and cawing angrily. The mother kite was flying round and round in circles, and was evidently sorely troubled in spirit. She had done something to offend the crows. Ere long she returned to her nest, whereupon the crows took to their wings, cawing more vociferously than ever. As soon as the kite had settled on the nest they again alighted on branches of the tree, and, each from a respectful distance, gave what the natives of Upper India call *gali galoj*. She tolerated for a time their vulgar abuse, then left the nest. This was the signal for all the crows to take to their wings. Some of them tried to attack her in the air. For a few minutes I watched them chasing her. After a little the attack began to flag, I, therefore, came to the conclusion that the *corvi* were recovering their mental equilibrium, and that the whole affair would quickly fizzle out, as such incidents usually do. Accordingly, I went on my way. Returning an hour later, I was surprised to find the crows still engaged in the attack. Moreover, the kite was not visible and the crows had grown bolder, for whereas previously they had abused the kite from a safe distance, some of them were now quite close to the nest. Being pressed for time, I was not able to stay and await developments. In the afternoon when I again passed the nest I saw no kite, but the tree was alive with crows, and part of the nest appeared to have been pulled down. The nestlings had probably been destroyed. Of this I was not able to make certain, for I was on my way to fulfil a social engagement. I was, I admit, sorely tempted to "cut" this, and nothing but the want of a good excuse prevented my doing so. "Dear Mrs. Burra Mem, I much regret that I was prevented from coming to your tennis party this afternoon by a domestic bereavement—of a kite," seemed rather unconvincing, so I went to the lawn-tennis party.

When I saw the nest the following morning it was a total wreck. There were still one or two crows hanging around, and while I was inspecting the ground beneath the scene of the tragedy they amused themselves by dropping sticks on my head. The crow is an ill-conditioned bird. I found, lying about on the ground, the *débris* of the nest, a number of kite's feathers, including six or seven of the large tail ones, and two crow's wings. These last furnished the clue to the behaviour of the crows. The kite must have attacked and killed a sickly crow, in order to provide breakfast for her young. This was, of course, an outrage on corvine society—an outrage which demanded speedy vengeance. Hence the gathering of the clans which I

THE INDIAN KITE. (MILVUS GOVINDA)

had witnessed the previous day. At first the crows were half afraid of the kite, and were content to call her names; but as they warmed up to their work they gained courage, and so eventually killed the kite, destroyed her nest, and devoured her young. Thus did they avenge the murder.

TWO LITTLE BIRDS

THERE is, hidden away in a corner of Northern India, a tiny orchard which may be likened to an oasis in the desert, because the trees which compose it are always fresh and green, even when the surrounding country is dry and parched. Last April two or three of the paradise flycatchers who were on their annual journey northward were tempted to tarry awhile in this orchard to enjoy the cool shade afforded by the trees. They found the place very pleasant, and insect life was so abundant that they determined to remain there during the summer. Thus it chanced that one morning, early in May, a cock flycatcher was perched on one of the trees, preening his feathers. A magnificent object was he amid the green foliage. The glossy black of his crested head formed a striking contrast to the whiteness of the remainder of his plumage. His two long median tail feathers, that hung down like satin streamers, formed an ornament more beautiful than the train of a peacock. He was so handsome that a hen flycatcher, who was sitting in a tree near by, resolved to make him wed her; but there was another hen living in the same orchard who was equally determined to secure the handsome cock as her mate. Even while the first hen was admiring him, her rival came up and made as if to show off her dainty chestnut plumage. This so angered the first hen that she attacked her rival. A duel then took place between the two little birds. It was not of long duration, for the second hen soon discovered that she was no match for the first, and deeming discretion to be the better part of valour, she flew away and left the orchard before she sustained any injury. Then the triumphant hen, flushed with victory, went up to the cock and said, "See what I have done for love of thee. I have driven away my rival. Wed me, I pray, for I am worthy of thee. Behold how beautiful I am." The cock looked at her as she stood there spreading her chestnut wings and saw that she was fair to gaze upon. He then fluttered his snowy pinions and sang a sweet little warble, which is the way a cock bird tells the lady of his choice that he loves her.

For the next few days these little birds led an idyllic existence. Free from care and anxiety, they disported themselves in that shady grove, now playing hide-and-seek among the foliage, now making graceful sweeps after their insect quarry, now pouring out the fulness of their love—the cock in sweet song and mellow warble, the hen in her peculiar twittering note. Their happiness was complete; never did the shadow of a cloud mar the sunshine of their springtime.

One day they were simultaneously seized by the impulse to build a nest. First a suitable site had to be chosen. After much searching and anxious consultation, mingled with love-making, they agreed upon the branch of a pear tree, some eight feet above the ground. During the whole of the following week they were busy seeking for grass stems, which they fastened to the branch of the tree by means of strands of cobweb. They did not hunt for material in company, as some birds do. The cock would go in one direction and the hen in another. Each, as it found a suitable piece of dried grass, or moss, or cobweb, or whatever it happened to be seeking, would dash back joyfully to the nest with it and weave it into the structure. Sometimes one bird would return while the other was at work on the nursery; the former would then sit near by and wait until the latter had finished.

At the end of the first day the nest appeared to the uninitiated eye merely a tangle of grass stems stuck on to the tree, but owing to the united efforts of the energetic little builders, it soon took definite shape. By the third day it was obvious that the nest was to have the form of an inverted cone firmly bound to the branch of the tree. The birds took the utmost care to make the nest circular. In order to ensure a smooth, round cavity they would sit in it and, with wings spread over the edge, turn their bodies round and round. At the end of about five days' steady work the nursery had assumed its final shape. But even then much remained to be done. The whole of the exterior had to be thickly covered with cobweb and little silky cocoons. This was two full days' work.

Great was the delight of the little birds when the last delicate filament had been added. Their joy knew no bounds. They would sit in the nest and cry out in pure delight. The whole orchard rang with their notes of jubilation. Then a little pinkish egg, spotted with red, appeared in the nest. This was followed, next day, by

another.   On the fifth day after its completion the
nursery contained the full clutch of four eggs.

Most carefully did the birds watch over their priceless
treasures.   Never for a moment did they leave them
unguarded ; one of the pair invariably remained sitting
on the nest, while the other went to look for food and
dissipate its exuberant energy in song or motion.   During the day the cock and hen shared equally the duties
of incubation, but the hen sat throughout the night
while the cock roosted in a tree hard by.   So healthy
were the little birds and so comfortably weary with the
labours of the day that they slept uninterruptedly all the
night through ; nor did they wake up when a human
being came with a lantern and inspected the nest.   Thus
some ten days passed.   But these were not days of
weariness, because the hearts of the little flycatchers were
full of joy.

Then a young bird emerged from one of the eggs.   It
was an unlovely, naked creature—all mouth and stomach.
But its parents did not think it ugly.   Its advent only
served to increase their happiness.   They were now able
to spend their large surplus of energy in seeking food
for it.

Ere long its brethen came out of their shells, and there
were then four mouths to feed ; so that the father and
mother had plenty to do, but they still found time in
which to sing.

Thus far everything had gone as merrily as a marriage
bell.   The happiness of those lovely little airy fairy
creatures was without alloy.   It is true that they sometimes had their worries and anxieties, as when a human

being chanced to approach the nest; but these were as fleeting as the tints in a sunset sky, and were half forgotten ere they had passed away. This idyllic existence was, alas, not destined to endure.

One day, when the man who kept guard over the orchard slumbered, a native boy entered it with the intention of stealing fruit. But the pears were yet green, and this angered the urchin. As he was about to leave the grove he espied the beautiful cock flycatcher sitting on the nest. The boy had no soul for beauty; he was not spell-bound by the beautiful sight that met his eyes. He went to the tree, drove away the sitting bird, tore down the branch on which the nest was placed and bore it off with its occupants in triumph, amid the distressed cries of the cock bird. These soon brought back the hen, and great was her lamentation when she found that that which she valued most in the world had gone. Her sorrow and rage knew no bounds. Poignant, too, was the grief of the cock bird, for he had been an eye-witness of the dastardly act. For a few hours all the joy seemed to have left the lives of those little birds. But they were too active, too healthy, too full of life to be miserable long. Soon the pleasantness of their surroundings began to manifest itself to them and soothe their sorrow, for the sun was still shining, the air was sweet and cool, the insects hummed their soft chorus, and their fellow-birds poured forth their joy. So the cock began to sing and said to his mate, " Be not cast down, the year is yet young, many suns shall come and go before the cold will drive us from this northern clime ; there is time for us to build another nest. Let us leave this

treacherous grove and seek some other place." The
hen found that these words were good. Thus did these
little birds forget their sorrow and grow as blithe and
gay as they had been before. But that orchard knew
them no more.

THE PARADISE FLYCATCHER

THE cock paradise flycatcher (*Terpsiphone paradisi*), when in full adult plumage, is a bird of startling beauty. I shall never forget the first occasion upon which I saw him. It was in the Himalayas when night was falling that I caught sight of some white, diaphanous-looking creature flitting about among the trees. In the dim twilight it looked ghostly in its beauty.

It is the two elongated, middle tail feathers which render the bird so striking. They look like white satin streamers and are responsible for the bird's many popular names, such as cotton - thief, ribbon - bird, rocket-bird. But this flycatcher has more than striking beauty to commend it to the naturalist; it is of surpassing interest from the point of view of biological theory. The cock is one of the few birds that undergo metamorphosis during adult life, and the species furnishes an excellent example of sexual dimorphism.

Since the day, some years back, when I first set eyes upon the bird, I determined to learn something of its habits; but I had to wait long before I was able to carry out my determination. It was not until I came to Lahore that I saw much of the species. Here let me say that the capital of the Punjab, unpromising as it looks at first sight, is, when one gets to know it, a veritable gold mine for the ornithologist.

Paradise flycatchers migrate there in great numbers in order to breed. They arrive at the end of April and at once commence nesting operations. Before describing these, let me, in order to enable non-ornithological readers to appreciate what follows, say a few words regarding the plumage of the bird. The young of both sexes are chestnut in colour, with the exception of a black head and crest and whitish under parts. This plumage is retained by the hen throughout life. After the autumn moult of the second year the two median tail feathers of the cock grow to a length of sixteen inches, that is to say, four times the length of the other tail feathers, and are retained till the following May or June, when they are cast. After the third autumn moult they again grow, and the plumage now begins to become gradually white, the wings and tail being the first portions to be affected by the change; thus the cock is for a time partly chestnut and partly white, and it is not until he emerges from the moult of his fourth autumn that all his feathers are white, with, of course, the exception of those of his head and crest. The bird retains this plumage until death. Cock birds breed in either chestnut or white plumage; this proves that the metamorphosis from chestnut to white takes place after the bird has attained maturity.

In Lahore this species nests in considerable numbers along the well-wooded banks of the Ravi. Since the birds keep to forest country it is not easy to follow their courting operations for any length of time; the birds engaged in courtship appear for a moment and then are lost to view among the foliage, but the species is certainly monogamous, and I think there can be but little doubt that the hen courts the cock quite as much as he courts her. On 28th April I was out with Mr. G. A. Pinto, and he saw a couple of hens chasing a cock in white plumage. Presently one of the hens drove away the other, then the cock showed off to the triumphant hen, expanding his wings and uttering a sweet little song, like the opening bars of that of the white-browed fantail flycatcher (*Rhipidura albifrontata*). I myself was not a witness of that incident, the birds not being visible from where I was standing at the time; but on 3rd June I saw a cock bird in chestnut plumage and a hen fighting; before long the birds disengaged themselves and the male flew off; then a cock in white plumage came up to the hen and gave her a bit of his mind. After this they both disappeared among the foliage. Presently I saw two hens chasing a chestnut-coloured cock. I do not understand the full significance of these incidents, but they tend to refute Charles Darwin's contention that there is competition among cocks for hens but none among hens for cocks, and to show that the hen takes an active part in courtship. To this I shall return.

It does not seem to be generally known that the cock paradise flycatcher is capable of emitting anything approaching a song. Thus Oates writes in *The Fauna of British India* of these flycatchers, "their notes are very harsh." This is true of the usual call, which is short, sharp, and harsh, something like the twitter of an angry sparrow. But in addition to this the cock has two tuneful calls. One resembles the commencement of the song of the white-browed fantail flycatcher, and the other is a sweet little warble of about four notes. I have repeatedly been quite close to the cock when thus singing and have seen his throat swell when he sang, so there can be no question as to the notes being his. He thus furnishes one of the many exceptions to the rule that brilliantly plumaged birds have no song.

The nest is a deepish cup, firmly attached to two or more slender branches; it is in shape like an inverted cone with the point prolonged as a stalk. It is composed chiefly of vegetable fibres and fine grass; these being coated outwardly by a thick layer of cobweb and small white cocoons. Let me take this opportunity of remarking that cobweb affords a most important building material to bird masons; it is their cement, and many species, such as sunbirds and flycatchers, use it most unsparingly.

The paradise flycatcher seems to delight to build in exposed situations, hence a great many of their nests come to grief, especially in the Punjab, where, if there be anything in phrenology, the bumps of destructiveness and cruelty must be enormously developed in every small boy.

The nesting habits of the paradise flycatcher have been described in detail in the preceding article. They are of considerable biological importance. I would lay especial stress on the active part in courtship played by the hen, the large share in incubation taken by the cock, and the change in the plumage of the cock bird from chestnut to white in the third year of his existence.

Darwin, as I have already pointed out, devoted much time and energy in trying to prove that there is in most species competition among males for females, and that these latter are in consequence able to exercise a selection. They choose the most brilliant and beautiful of their numerous suitors. Thus we have what he calls sexual selection, or, as I should prefer to call it, feminine selection. On this theory the poor cock exercises no selection; any decrepit old hen is good enough for him! He is all eagerness, while the hen is *blasé* and indifferent. This theory is, I submit, improbable on *a priori* grounds. It is certainly opposed to human experience, and is, I believe, not borne out by animal behaviour.

I have paid some attention to the subject lately, and am convinced that in most cases the desire of the hen for the cock is as great as the desire of the latter for the hen. It was only this morning that I watched two hen orioles trying to drive each other away, while the cock was in a tree near by.

To repeat what I have already said, the hen courts the cock quite as much as he courts her. When a pair of birds mate they are mutually attracted to one another. That there is such a thing as sexual selection I am convinced, but I do not believe that this selection is confined to the hens. The hen selects the best cock she can get to pair with her, while the cock selects the best hen available.

I speak here of monogamous species; among polygamous ones there must of necessity be considerable competition for hens.

The second point upon which I desire to lay stress is the active part taken by the cock paradise flycatcher in incubation. This, again, is, I believe, nothing very uncommon, even in sexually dimorphic species, for I have myself put a cock minvet (*Pericrocotus peregrinus*) off the nest. Yet this fact seems to dispose of Wallace's theory that the more sombre hues of the hen are due to her greater need of protection, since she alone is supposed to incubate.

As a matter of fact, a bird sitting on a nest is not, in my opinion, exposed to any special danger, for it seems that birds of prey as a rule only attack flying objects.

Finally, there is the extraordinary metamorphosis undergone by the cock in his fourth year. It is difficult to see how this can have been caused by the preference of the hen for white cock birds, since a great many chestnut ones are observed to breed; the dimorphism must, therefore, have originated late in the life history of the species, and although a hen bird might prefer a white to a chestnut husband, it is difficult to believe that she would prefer a skewbald one, and this skewbald state must have been an ancestral stage if we believe that the transition is due to feminine selection of white birds. I may be asked, "If you decline to believe that the hen has greater need of protection than the cock, how do you account for the phenomena of sexual dimorphism, and if it is not sexual selection which has caused the white plumage of the cock paradise flycatcher to arise, what is it?"

M

This article has already attained such a length that even had I complete explanations to offer I could not set them forth in this place. I must content myself with giving what I believe to be the key to the solution of the problem. I think that there is little doubt that what a bird looks for in its mate is, *not beauty or brilliance of plumage, but vigour and strength.* If beauty is a correlative character to strength, then the hen selects the most beautiful of the cocks willing to mate with her, not because of his beauty, but on account of his strength; likewise the cock. Now there is a very intimate connection between the generative cells and the body cells, and the male element tends to dissipate energy and the female element to conserve it. Thus it is that the general tendency of the cock is to become gaily coloured and to grow plumes and other ornaments, while the tendency of the hen is to remain of comparatively sombre hue.

BUTCHER BIRDS

BUTCHER birds are so called because they are reputed to have a habit of impaling on thorns their larger victims, or as much of them as they, owing to want of accommodation, are incapable of eating at the time of the murder. A bush which displays a number of impaled victims— young birds, lizards, locusts, and the like—is supposed, by a stretch of the ornithological imagination, to look like a butcher's shop. All that is wanted to perfect the illusion is a sign-board, bearing the legend " Lanius vittatus, Purveyor of Meat." I must here admit, with characteristic honesty, that I have never set eyes upon such a butcher's shop, or larder, as it should be called, for the shrike does not sell his wares—he merely stores them for personal consumption. Nor have I even seen a shrike impale a victim. My failure cannot, I think, be attributed to lack of observation ; for I never espy one of these miniature birds of prey without watching it attentively, in the hope that it will oblige me by acting as all books on ornithology tell me shrikes do. Every butcher bird I have witnessed engaged in *shikar* has pounced down upon its insect quarry from a suitable perch, seized the luckless victim upon the ground, immediately carried it back to its perch and devoured it then and there. I have seen this operation repeated scores of times. I, therefore, think I am justified in suggesting that the habit of keeping a larder is probably restricted to the larger species of shrike, and that these only impale their victim when there is still something of it left over, after they have eaten so much that for the time being they cannot possibly stow away any more. Jerdon, I notice, makes no mention of ever having seen a butcher bird behave in the orthodox manner. Colonel Cunningham, who is a very close observer of bird life, says, as the result of a long sojourn in India, that shrikes " do not seem very often to impale their victims, probably because these are usually easily broken up ; but when they have secured a lizard they sometimes fix it down upon a stout thorn so as to have a point of resistance whilst working at the hard, tough skin." If any who read these lines have seen a shrike's larder, either in India or in England, I should esteem it a great favour if they would furnish me with some account of it.

Let me not be mistaken. I do not say that butcher birds never keep larders, for they undoubtedly do ; of this I am satisfied. Thus Mr. E. H. Aitken says of the shrike : " It sits upright on the top of a bush or low tree, commanding a good expanse of open, grassy land, and watches for anything which it may be able to surprise and murder—a large grasshopper, a small lizard, or a creeping field mouse. Sometimes it sees a possible chance in a flock of small birds absorbed in searching for grass seeds. Then it slips from its watch-tower and, gliding softly down, pops into the midst of them without warning, and forgetting all about the true nature of its deep plantar tendons, strikes its talons into the nearest. No other bird I know of makes its attack in this way except the birds of prey. The little bird shrieks and struggles, but the cruel shrike holds fasts and hammers at the victim's head with its strong beak until it is dead, then flies away with it to some thorn bush which is its larder. There it hangs it up on a thorn and leaves it to get tender. . . . This is no fable, I have seen the bird do it." Again, the Rev. C. D. Cullen, with whom I have enjoyed many an ornithological ramble in England and on the continent of Europe, informs me that once in Surrey he came upon a shrike's larder, and on that occasion the " shop " consisted of the legs of a young green finch.

The usual food, then, of the butcher bird appears to be small insects. When a suitable opportunity offers, the larger species will attack a lizard or a young or sickly bird, especially a bird in a cage. Of the rufous-backed shrike Mr. Benjamin Aitken writes : " It will come down at once to a cage of small birds exposed at a window, and I once had an amadavat killed and partly eaten through the wires by one of these shrikes, which I saw in the act with my own eyes. The next day I caught the shrike in a large basket which I set over the cage of amadavats." But, of course, it is one thing to catch a bird in a cage and another to capture it in the open. Shrikes are savage enough for any murder, but most little birds are too sharp for them.

Fifteen species of shrike occur in India. The commonest are, perhaps, the Indian grey shrike (*Lanius lahtora*) and the bay-backed shrike (*Lanius vittatus*).

The latter is the one that frequents our gardens. He is not a large bird, being about the size of a bulbul. The head and back of the neck are a pretty grey. The back is chestnut-maroon, shading off to whitish near the tail. There is a broad black streak running across the forehead and through the eye, giving the bird a grim, sinister aspect. The breast and lower parts are white; the wings and tail black, or rather appear black when the bird is at rest. During flight the pinions display a conspicuous white bar, and the white outer tail feathers also come into view. The stout beak is black, and the upper mandible projects downwards over the lower one. This further adds to the ferocity of the bird's mien. It is impossible to mistake a butcher bird; look out for its grey head, broad, black eyebrow, and white breast.

The usual note of the shrike is a harsh cry, but during the breeding season, that is to say, from March to July, the cock is able to produce quite a musical song.

At all times the butcher bird is a great mimic. I am indebted to a correspondent for the following graphic account of his histrionic performances: " Of late one of these birds has daily perched himself on a *neem* tree in my compound and treated me to much music. His hours of practice are early in the morning and at sunset. He begins with his natural harsh notes, and then launches out into mimicry. I gave him a patient hearing this morning, and he treated me to the following : the lapwing, the sparrow-hawk, the partridge, the Brahminy minah, the kite, the honeysucker, the hornbill (of these parts), the scream of the green parrot, and the cry of a chicken when being carried off by a kite."

The nests of the various species of shrike resemble one another very closely. Speaking generally, the nest is a neatly made, thick-walled, somewhat deep cup. All manner of material is pressed into service—grass, roots, wool, hair, leaves, feathers, pieces of rag, paper, fine twigs, and straw. The whole forms a compact structure firmly held together by cobweb, which is the cement ordinarily utilised by bird masons.

The nursery is usually situated in a small tree, a thorny one for preference, in the fork of a branch, or the angle that a branch makes with the main stem. Seen from below it looks likes a little mass of rubbish. As a rule one or two pieces of rag hang down from it and betray its presence to the egg-collector.

The normal clutch of eggs is four. The ground colour of these is cream, pale greenish, or grey, and there is towards the large end a zone of brown or purplish blotches.

The shrike is not a shy bird. I have sat within eight feet of a nest and watched the parents feeding their young. No notice was taken of me, but a large lizard that appeared on the branch on which the nest was placed was savagely attacked. The young seem to be fed chiefly on large green caterpillars.

Newly fledged butcher birds differ considerably from the adults, and while in the transition stage are sometimes rather puzzling to the ornithologist.

DUCKS

"THE duck," says a writer in the *Spectator*, "is a person who seldom gets his deserts." As regards myself I cannot but admit the truth of this assertion. I mean, not that I am a duck, but that I have returned that bird evil for good. He has given me much pleasure, and I have either eaten or shot him as a *quid pro quo*.

One of the greatest delights of my early youth was to feed the ducks that lived on the Serpentine. How vividly do I remember the joy that the operation gave me! In the first place, I was allowed to enter the kitchen—that Forbidden Land of childhood's days, presided over by a fearsome tyrant, yclept the cook—and witness dry bread being cut up into pieces of a size supposed to be suited to the mastication of ducks. The bread thus cut up would be placed in a paper bag and borne off by me in triumph to the upper regions. Then my sister and I, accompanied by the governess, would toddle up Sloane Street, through Lowndes Square, past the great French Embassy, into Hyde Park, along Rotten Row, and thus up to that corner of the Serpentine where the ducks were wont to congregate. There, amid a chorus of quacks, the bread would be thrown, piece by piece, to the ever-hungry ducks. The writer in the

Spectator states that "the domestic duck, unlike his wild brother, is a materialist, and where dinner is concerned is decidedly greedy." The avidity with which the ducks used to make for those pieces of dry bread certainly bears out this statement. Every time a crust was thrown on to the water there would be a wild scramble for it. One individual, more fortunate than the others, would secure it, and, sprinting away from his comrades, would endeavour to swallow it whole. I have said that the pieces of bread were cut up into portions of a size supposed to be convenient for the mastication of a duck; but, if the truth must be told, the cook invariably over-estimated the size of the bird's gullet; hence the frantic muscular efforts to induce them to descend "red lane." It is a miracle that not one of those ducks shared the sad fate of Earl Godwin.

Some of them must certainly have lost the epithelial lining of the œsophagus in their desperate efforts to dispose of those pieces of dry bread. An exceptionally unmanageable morsel would be dropped again into the water, and there would be a second scramble for it. By this time, however, it would have become so much softened as to be comparatively easy to swallow. How we used to enjoy watching the efforts of those ducks to negotiate the pieces of bread! We were, of course, blissfully ignorant of the unnaturalness of the process. Our governess used to read, in preference to natural history, fiction of the class in which the fortunate scullery-maid always marries a Duke. Thus it was that my sister and I knew nothing of the wonderful structure of the duck's beak. We were not aware that the mandibles were lamellated or toothed to form a most efficient sieve. We were not acquainted with the fact that the natural food of the duck is composed of small, soft substances, that as the bird puts its head under water it catches up its breath to suck in the soft substances that may be floating by, that these become broken up as they pass through the duck's patent filter, only those that are approved being retained and swallowed. But the want of this knowledge did not diminish by one jot or tittle our enjoyment. When all the bread was disposed of, we would inflate and " pop " the paper bag—a performance which gave us nearly as much pleasure as feeding the ducks.

As I grew older I came to regard the feeding of ducks as a childish amusement, and in no way suited to one who had attained the dignity of stand-up collars. So, for some years, I took but little interest in the birds, except on the occasions when one confronted me at table.

It has again become a pleasure to feed ducks, but I fear that, in spite of this, I shoot them more often than I feed them. I must confess that, when I see a great company of the quacking community, the sportsman in me gets the upper hand of the naturalist, the lust of killing prevails over the love of observation. I know of few greater pleasures than to spend a morning at a well-stocked *jhil* on a superb winter's day in Northern India, accompanied, of course, by a number of fellow-sportsmen ; for duck shooting is poor sport for a single gun. With but one man after them it is the ducks rather than the human being who enjoy the sport. But,

given three or four companions, what better sport is
there than that afforded by a day on a well-stocked *jhil*?
At a preconcerted signal the various shooters, each in
his boat, put off from different parts of the bank of the
lake and make for the middle, which is black with a
great company of quack-quacks, composed chiefly
of white-eyed pochards, gadwalls, and spotted-bills.
Suddenly a number of duck take alarm and get up;
then the fun begins. For half an hour or more one
enjoys a succession of good sporting shots; the firing is
so constant that one's gun grows almost too hot to hold.
Soon, however, all the duck that are not shot down
betake themselves to some other *jhil*, and only the
coots remain.

Excellent sport though duck shooting be, I am thankful
to say that in these latter days my acquaintance with
the duck tribe is not confined to shooting and eating
members of it. I occasionally have the opportunity of
coming into more friendly relations with it.

The duck is a bird worth knowing. He is a fowl of
character, a creature that commands not only our respect,
but our affection. He makes an excellent pet, as any one
may find out by purchasing some bazaar ducks.

Some years ago the cook of the Superintendent of
Police of a certain district in the United Provinces purchased a couple of these birds. When bought they were
in an emaciated condition, and it was the intention of
the cook to fatten them up and then set them before his
master. But before the fattening process was completed
the small sons of the policeman took a great fancy to
the birds, and the birds reciprocated the fancy. The

result was that their lives were spared, and they became friends of the family. They went everywhere with the children, and used even to accompany them when on tour with their father. They were allowed to enter the tents as though they were dogs, and in return used to permit the children to do anything they pleased with them. They even submitted to being carried about like dolls. Most amusing was it to see the good-natured boredom on a duck's face as a small boy staggered along with it tightly clasped in his arms. Its expression would say more plainly than words, " I don't altogether relish this, but I know the child means well."

Nor was this behaviour in any way exceptional. A better-disposed creature than the duck does not exist. " I have kept and closely watched hundreds of ducks," writes Mr. S. M. Hawkes, " but I never saw them fight with each other, nor ever knew a duck the aggressor in a dispute with some other kind of fowl." Yet the duck is no coward. The drake is a warrior every inch of him, constant in affection, and violent in love and wrath. If the adult duck is so lovable, how much more so is the duckling ! What a source of delight are those golden fluff balls to a child. On seeing them for the first time nine out of ten children will cry—

But I want one to play with—Oh I want
A little yellow duck to take to bed with me !

A DETHRONED MONARCH

THE eagle is a bird that deserves much sympathy, for he has seen better times. Until a few years ago the pride of place among the fowls of the air was always given to the eagle. "Which eagle?" you ask. I reply, "*The* eagle." The poets, who have ever been the bird's trumpeters, know but one eagle upon which they lavish such epithets as "the imperial bird," "the royal eagle," "the monarch bird," "lord of land and sea," "the wide-ruling eagle," "the prince of all the feathered kind," "the king of birds," "the bird of heaven," "the Olympic eagle," "the bold imperial bird of Jove," and so on, *ad nauseam*.

The eagle of the poets was truly regal. But somebody discovered, one day, that this bird is, like the phœnix, a mythical creature. Eagles do exist—many species of them—but they are very ordinary creatures, in no way answering to the description of the poet's pet fowl. This, of course, is not the fault of the eagles. They are not to blame because the bards have, with one accord, combined to idealise them. Nevertheless, men, now that they have found out the truth, seem to bear a grudge against the eagle. They are not content with dethroning him, they must needs throw mud at

173

him. It is the present custom to vilify the eagle, to speak of him as though he were an opponent at an election, to dub him a cowardly carrion feeder, little if anything better than a common vulture. Let us, therefore, give the poor out-at-elbows bird an innings to-day and see what we can do for him.

But how are we to recognise him when we see him? This is indeed a problem. There is a feature by which the true eagles may be distinguished from all other birds of prey, namely, the feathered tarsus. The true eagles alone among the *raptores* decline to go about with bare legs; their "understandings" are feathered right down to the toe. Thus may they be recognised.

This method of identification is on a par with that of catching a bird by placing a small quantity of salt upon its tail. Eagles show no readiness to come and have their legs inspected. There is, I fear, no feature whereby the tyro can distinguish an eagle as it soars overhead high in the heavens. Nothing save years of patient observation can enable the naturalist to identify any particular bird of prey at sight. Colour is, alas! no guide. The *raptores* are continually changing their plumage. It were as easy to identify a woman by the colour of her frock as a bird of prey by the hues of its plumage. We read of one eagle that it is tawny rufous, of another that it is rufous tawny, of a third that it is tawny buff. The surest method of distinguishing the various birds of prey is by their flight; but is it possible to describe the peculiar flap of the wings of one eagle, and the particular angle at which another carries its pinions as it sails along? The length

of the tail is a guide, but by no means an infallible one.
The shikra, the sparrow-hawk, the kestrel, and the kite
are long-tailed birds, the caudal appendage accounting
for half their total length. In the eagles the tail is
considerably shorter in proportion to the size of the
bird. Thus the female of the golden eagle (*Aquila
chrysætus*)—which, *en passant*, is not gold in colour, but
dirty whitish brown—is 40 inches long, while the tail is
but 14 inches. The vultures have yet shorter tails in
proportion to their size. If, therefore, you see soaring
overhead a big bird of prey, looking like a large kite,
with a moderate tail and curved rather than straight
wings, that bird is probably an eagle. So much, then,
for the appearance of our dethroned monarch ; it now
behoves us to consider his character and habits. There
are many species of eagle, each of which has its own
peculiar ways, hence it is impossible for the naturalist
to generalise concerning them. In this respect he is
not so fortunate as the poet. Let us briefly consider
two species, one belonging to the finer type of eagle
and the other to the baser sort.

Bonelli's eagle (*Hieraetus fasciatus*), or the crestless
hawk eagle as Jerdon calls him, is perhaps the nearest
approach of any to the poet's eagle. This fine bird is
common on the Nilgiris, but rare in Madras. It is said
to disdain carrion ; it preys on small mammals and
birds of all sizes. It takes game birds by preference,
but when hungry does not draw the line at the crow. If
it has hunted all day without obtaining the wherewithal
to fill its belly, it repairs to the grove of trees in which
all the crows of the neighbourhood roost. As the sun

sinks in the heavens the crows arrive in straggling flocks. Suddenly the eagle dashes into the midst of them and, before the crows have realised what has happened, one of them is being carried away in the eagle's talons. Then the *corvi* fill the welkin with their cries of distress. It is very naughty of the eagle to prey upon crows in this way, because by so doing it mocks the theory of protective colouration. No one can maintain that our friend *Corvus splendens* is protectively coloured, that is to say, so coloured as to be inconspicuous. No one but a blind man can fail to see a crow as he steadily flaps his way through the air. No one can deny that the bird flourishes, in spite of the fact that eagles eat him, and that his plumage is as conspicuous as the blazer of the Lady Margaret Boat Club at Cambridge. If, as the theory teaches, it is of paramount importance to a bird to be inconspicuous, why was not the whole clan of *corvi* swept off the face of the earth long ago?

We have, in conclusion, to consider an eagle of the baser sort. The Indian tawny eagle (*Aquila vindhiana*), which is the commonest eagle in India, will serve as an example. This bird eats anything in the way of flesh that it can obtain. If the opportunity offers, it will pounce upon a squirrel, a small bird, a lizard, or a frog; but it is a comparatively sluggish creature, and so robs other *raptores* in preference to catching its own quarry. Most birds of prey are robbers. This the falconer knows, and profits by his knowledge. He first captures some small bird of prey, such as a white-eyed buzzard. Having tied up two or three of its wing feathers so that it cannot fly far, he attaches to its feet a bundle of feathers, from which hang a number of fine hair nooses. He then flies this lure bird. Every bird of prey in the neighbourhood espies it and, seeing the bundle of feathers and remarking the laboured flight, jumps to the conclusion that it is carrying booty, and promptly gives chase with the object of relieving it of its burden. The first robber to arrive is caught in one of the nooses.

The tawny eagle is not above feeding upon carrion. It has not the pluck of Bonelli's eagle, but is apparently not the contemptible coward it is made out to be by some writers. A few weeks ago I noticed, high up in a *farash* tree, the platform of sticks and branches that does duty for the nest of this species. I sent my climber to find out what was in the nest. While he was handling the two eggs it contained, the mother eagle swooped down upon him, scratched his head severely, and flew off with his turban. As she sped away, her prize attracted the notice of some kites, who at once attacked her. In the *mêlée* which ensued, the *puggaree* dropped to the ground, to the joy of its lawful owner and the disgust of the combatants. I must add that I was not an eye-witness of the encounter; I however saw the marks of the bird's claws on my climber's scalp.

N

BIRDS IN THE RAIN

THERE are occasions when one is tempted
to wish that one were a bird, for the fowls
of the air are spared many of the troubles
which we poor terrestrial creatures have
to endure.

Most of us in India have received a telegram ordering
us off to some far-away station ; then, when distracted
by the worry and bustle of packing ; when the hideous
noises of the Indian railway station "get on the
nerves" ; as we sit in the dusty, jolting train, we begin
to envy the birds who are able to annihilate distance,
who have no boxes to pack up, no baggage to go astray,
no bills to pay, no *chits* to write, no cards to leave, no
time-table to worry through, no trains to lose, no
connections to miss, but have simply to take to their
wings and away.

Most of us, again, have been caught in the rain.
As the watery contents of the clouds slowly but surely
percolated through our clothes, as our boots grew heavier
and heavier until the water oozed out at every step, we
must have envied the birds. They know naught of
rheumatism or ague. Their clothes do not spoil in the
rain. They wear no boots to become waterlogged.
Their wings rarely become heavy or sodden. For them

the rain is a huge joke. They enjoy the falling rain-drops as keenly as a man enjoys his morning shower-bath. There is no bath like the rain bath, and if the drops do fall very heavily there is always shelter to be taken.

It is of course possible for birds to have too much rain; but this does not often happen in India, except occasionally in the monsoon.

As I write this it is pouring "cats and dogs," and sitting in a tree not five yards away from the window are a couple of crows thoroughly enjoying the blessings which Jupiter Pluvius is showering down upon them. I am high up, seventy or eighty feet above the level of the ground, and can therefore look down upon the crows. They are perched on the ends of the highest branches, determined not to miss a drop of the rain. One of them is not quite satisfied with his position; he espies another bough which seems more exposed, so to this branch he flies, although it is so slender that it can scarce support him. Nevertheless he hangs on to his swaying perch and opens out his wings and flaps his tail—does, in fact, everything in his power to make the most of the passing tropical shower. The other crow has caught sight of me, and thinks he will stare me out, so sits motionless with his eye fixed on mine, while the rain pours upon him and falls off his tail in a little waterfall. Occasionally he gives his friend an answering "squawk," and then shakes his feathers, and is altogether enjoying himself; he is as jolly as the proverbial sandboy. In other trees near by sit more crows, and, so far as one can judge, each seems to have taken up a position in which he is likely to secure the maximum of rain. All round there is ample shelter; there are numerous ledges, outhouses, and verandahs, in any of which the crows could obtain shelter if they desired it. Shelter? Not a bit of it, they revel in the rain.

Two pied wagtails fly by, chasing one another glee-fully in the pouring rain; they too are regular "wet bobs."

On the telegraph wires hard by the king-crows sit with their tails projecting horizontally so as to catch as much of the downpour as possible. The dragon-flies are seeking their prey regardless of the rain; this is somewhat surprising, when we consider that to them a drop of rain must bear about the same relation as a glass of water does to a human being. As they are hunting, it is obvious that the minute creatures on which they feed must also be out in the rain, although every drop contains quite sufficient water in which to drown them.

The mortality of small insects in a heavy fall of rain must be enormous. What a strange sight a shower must look to an insect! Each drop must seem like a waterspout.

Are tiny insects aware that the falling drops are fraught with danger to them? Do they attempt to dodge them? I think not. They can know nothing of death or of the danger of drowning. They probably fly about as usual in the rain in blissful ignorance of the harm that threatens them. Some escape unscathed, but others less fortunate are overwhelmed as in a flood, and in a few minutes their little spark of life is extinguished.

But to return to the birds. They are all making the most of the downpour, ruffling their feathers so that the water shall penetrate to the skin.

But the rain is more to the birds than a very pleasant form of bath. It is for them a *mi-carême*, a water carnival, an hour of licence when every bird—even the oldest and most staid—may throw appearances to the wind, when it is " quite the thing " to look dishevelled.

What a transformation does a shower of rain effect in the myna. As a rule the bird looks as smart as a lifeguardsman ; its uniform is so spick and span that the veriest martinet could find no fault with it. But after the rain has been falling for ten minutes the myna looks as disreputable as a babbler. A shower is the signal for all the birds to let themselves go and have a spree. No bird then minds how untidy it is, for it knows that there is none to point the finger of scorn at it ; all are in the same boat, or, at any rate, in the same shower of rain. So each one makes the most of the period of licence. The most staid birds splash about in puddles and revel in the experience in much the same way as a child enjoys paddling on the seashore.

And when the rain is over, what a shaking and preening of feathers there is ! What a general brushing up ! The bird world seems for a time to have turned itself into a toilet club. Presently, the last arcana of the toilet being completed, the birds come forth looking as fresh and sweet as an English meadow when the sun shines upon it after a summer shower.

Then there are all the good things which the rain

brings with it.   How luscious and sweet the fruit must taste when the raindrops have washed away all the dust and other impurities with defile it.   What a multitude of edible creeping things does a shower bring forth.   In England it causes to emerge all manner of grubs and worms which before had been lurking in their burrows.   In India is it not the rain that ushers in the red-letter day for insectivorous birds—the day that witnesses the swarming of the "white ants"?   What a feast do these myriads of termites provide for the feathered things.   In addition to these there is all the multitude of winged and crawling insects which the rain brings to life as if by magic.   How badly would the birds fare but for the *barsath* which brings forth these insects, upon which they are able to feed their young.

Perhaps the hoopoes most of all appreciate the rain, for it makes the ground so delightfully soft; they are then able with such ease to plunge their long beaks into the earth and extract all manner of hidden treasures which are usually most difficult of access.

Is there anything in the world more complete than the happiness of birds in a shower of rain ?

THE WEAVER BIRD

THE weaver bird has, thanks to its marvellous nest, a world-wide reputation. It is related to our ubiquitous friend the house sparrow, and is known to men of science as *Ploceus baya*.

Except at the breeding season, the weaver bird looks rather like an overgrown sparrow, and frequently passes as such. But the cock decks himself out in gay attire when he goes a-courting. The feathers of his head become golden, while his breast turns bright yellow if he be an elderly gentleman, or rusty red if he still possess the fire of youth.

Weaver birds are found all over India. In most parts they seem to shun the haunts of man, but in Burma they frequent gardens. Jerdon mentions a house in Rangoon which had at one time over one hundred weaver birds' nests suspended from the thatch of the roof! In India proper the favourite site for a nest is a tree that overhangs water. Toddy palms are most commonly chosen, but in Northern India, where palms are but rarely seen, a *babul* tree is usually utilised.

Weaver birds or bayas, as they are invariably called by Hindustani-speaking people, live almost exclusively on grain, hence they are easy birds to keep in captivity. Given a commodious aviary and plenty of grass, captive bayas amuse themselves by weaving their wonderful nests. They are, however, not very desirable as pets if they have to share a cage with other birds, for, as Colonel Cunningham remarks, " every weaver bird appears to be possessed by an innate desire to hammer in the head of his neighbour." To this the neighbour is apt to take exception, so that unpleasantness ensues.

Natives frequently train bayas to do all manner of tricks.

The man with performing birds is quite an institution in India. Parrots, bayas, and pigeons are most frequently trained.

A very effective trick, which is performed alike by parrots and weaver birds, is the loading and firing of a miniature cannon. First the bird places some grains of powder in the muzzle of the cannon, then it rams these home with a ramrod. It next takes a lighted match from its master, which it applies to the touch-hole. The result is a report loud enough to scare every crow in the neighbourhood, but the little baya will remain perched on the gun, having apparently thoroughly enjoyed the performance.

The nest of the baya is one of the most wonderful things in nature. Description is unnecessary. Every one who has been in India has seen dozens of the hanging flask-shaped structures, while those who know not the Gorgeous East must be acquainted with the nest from pictures.

On account of its champagne-bottle shaped nest, the

weaver is sometimes known as the bottle bird ; I have also heard it called the hedge sparrow.

It makes no attempt to conceal its exquisitely woven nest. It relies for protection on inaccessibility, not concealment. Every animal *badmash* can see the nest, but cannot get at it. It hangs sufficiently high to be out of reach of all four-footed creatures. The ends of the entrance passage are frayed out so as to baffle all attempts on the part of squirrels and lizards to reach the treasures hidden away in it.

Both cock and hen work at the nest, the cock being the more industrious. The fibres of which it is composed are not found ready-made. The birds manufacture them out of the tall elephant grass which is so common in India. The weaver alights on one of the nearly upright blades and seizes with its beak a neighbouring blade near the base and makes a notch in it ; it next seizes the edge of the blade above the notch and jerks its head away. By this means it strips off a thin strand of the leaf ; it then proceeds to tear off in a similar manner a second strand, retaining the first one in its beak ; in precisely the same way a third and perhaps a fourth strand are stripped off. The tearing process is not always continued to the extreme end of the blade ; the various strands sometimes remain attached to the tip of the blade. The force with which the bird flies away usually suffices to complete the severance ; sometimes, however, it is not effected so easily, and the bird is pulled back and swings in the air suspended by the strands it holds in its bill. Nothing daunted, the weaver makes a second attempt to fly away, and if this is not successful, continues until its efforts are crowned with success.

The grass which is used in nest construction is impregnated with silicon to such an extent that I experienced considerable difficulty in extricating from my pocket some of the fibres which, on one occasion, I took home with me. The material is thus eminently suitable for weaving purposes.

The fibres first collected are securely wound round the branch or leaf from which the nest will hang. The fibres added subsequently are plaited together until a stalk four or five inches long is formed ; this is then expanded into a bell-shaped structure. The bell constitutes the roof of the nursery. When the roof is completed a loop is constructed across its base, so that the nest at this stage may be likened to an inverted basket with a handle.

Up to this point the cock and hen do the same kind of work, both fetch strips of grass or of palm leaves and weave these into the structure of the nest. But when once the loop or cross-bar is completed the hen takes up a position on it and makes the cock do all the bringing of material. She henceforth works from the interior of the nest and he from the exterior.

They push the fibres through the walls to one another. Thus the work progresses very rapidly. On one side of the loop the bell is closed up so as to form a chamber in which the eggs are laid, and the other half is prolonged into a neck, which becomes the entrance to the nest. This may be nearly a foot long ; six inches is, however, a more usual length.

The entrance to the nursery is thus from below.   The way the owners shoot vertically upwards into it, with closed wings, without perceptibly shaking it is really marvellous.

Nest construction obviously gives the little builders great pleasure.   They frequently build supernumerary nests, purely from the joy of building.   Each time the cock bird approaches the nest with a beakful of material he cries out with delight.   Every now and again in the midst of weaving material into the structure of the nest he bursts into song.

Weaver birds usually build in company ; ten or a dozen different nests being found in the same tree.   As each little craftsman is in a very excited state, fights between neighbouring cocks frequently ensue, but these are never of a serious nature.   I was once the witness of an amusing piece of wickedness on the part of a cock baya.   The bird in question flew to a branch near the nest belonging to another pair of weaver birds who were absent.   After contemplating it for a little he flew to the nest, and having deliberately wrenched away a piece of it with his beak, made off with the stolen property and worked it into his own nest !   Four times did he visit his neighbour's nest and commit larceny ; two of the stolen strands he utilised and the remaining ones fell to the ground.   I am inclined to think that the thief was actuated by motives of jealousy ; for he deliberately dropped some of the stolen material on to the ground and extracted it from the place at which the nest was attached to its branch, thus weakening its attachment.   The victim of the outrage on his return did not appear to notice that anything was amiss.

Not the least interesting feature of the nest is the clay which is studded about it in lumps. In one nest Jerdon found no fewer than six of these lumps, weighing in all three ounces. The clay has, I think, three uses: it helps to balance the nest, it prevents it being blown about by every gust of wind, and keeps it steady while the bird is entering it.

A story is abroad, and is repeated in nearly every popular book on ornithology, to the effect that the weaver bird sticks fireflies on these lumps of clay, and thus illuminates the nursery, or renders it terrifying to predacious creatures. Jerdon scoffs at this firefly story, and I, too, am unable to accept it. Nevertheless it is so universally believed by the natives of India that there must be some foundation for it.

Some time ago a correspondent living on the West Coast of India informed me that weaver birds are very abundant in that part of the country, that their nests are everywhere to be seen, and that he had noticed fireflies stuck into many of them. He asked if I could explain their presence. I suggested in reply that he had made a mistake and requested him to look carefully next nesting season, that is to say in August, and, if he came upon a single nest on to which a firefly was stuck, to take it down, fireflies and all, and send it to me at my expense. Since then August has come and gone thrice, and I have heard nothing from my correspondent! Thus it is that I am still among those that disbelieve the firefly story.

My theory is that the bird brings the clay to the nest in its bill in a moist condition. Now wet clay retains moisture for some time and would shine quite brightly in the moonlight, so might easily be mistaken for a firefly. Unfortunately the weaver bird is not common where I am now stationed, so that I have not had an opportunity of putting this theory to the test. I have, however, noticed how the nests built by solitary wasps shine when the clay that composes them is wet.

The natives of Northern India attribute great medicinal value to the nest of the weaver bird. They assert that a baby will never suffer from boils if it be once washed in water in which a weaver bird's nest has been boiled!

A great many half-finished weaver birds' nests are seen in India. Most of these are the work of the cock, who thus amuses himself while his wife is incubating. A few are nests which have gone wrong, nests which do not balance nicely and so have not been completed.

Two eggs are usually laid; they are pure white and without any gloss. On these the hen sits very closely. On one occasion Hume took home a very fine specimen of the nest and hung it from one of a pair of antlers on his dining-room wall. Three days later the inmates of the bungalow became aware of a very unpleasant odour, which was traced to the nest. On taking it down it was found to contain a female baya dead upon two dead half-hatched chicks.

GREEN PARROTS

G REEN parrots, as the long-tailed paroquets of India are popularly called, although fairly abundant during the cold weather, cannot be said to be common birds in Madras. This is a small mercy, for which all Madrassis should be duly thankful. The green parrot is one of those good things of which it is possible to have too much. Where the beautiful birds are not too plentiful they are always greatly admired and considered most pleasing additions to the landscape ; where they abound most people find it difficult to speak of them in parliamentary language.

The Punjab is the happy hunting-ground of green parrots. I am now in a station where these birds probably outnumber the crows, where we are literally steeped in green parrots, where we hear nothing else all day long save their screeches and chuckles.

Green parrots owe their unpopularity to their mischievousness and their noisiness. " In their malignant love of destruction and mischief," writes Colonel Cunningham, " they run crows very hard, and seem only to fall short of that standard through the happy ordinance that their mental development has halted a good way behind that of their rivals. They are, therefore, incapable of devising such manifold and elaborate schemes of mischief

THE GREY-NECKED CROW. (CORVUS SPLENDENS)

as the crows work out, but in so far as intent and dis-
interested love of evil goes, there is not a pin to choose
between them. They take the same heart-whole delight
in destruction for destruction's sake, and find the same
bliss in tormenting and annoying other living things."
While fully endorsing the above, I feel constrained to
remark that the parrot is no fool ; he may not be quite
as 'cute as an Indian crow, but he is gifted with sufficient
brain-power for all practical purposes. If the green
parrot is less harmfully mischievous than the crow he is
far more offensively noisy. He is able to produce an
almost endless variety of sounds, but unfortunately there
is not a single one among them all which by any
stretch of the imagination can be called musical.

All species of green parrots have similar habits. All
are gregarious and feed almost exclusively on fruit and
seeds. They do much damage to the crops, destroying
more than they eat, since they have a way of breaking
off a head of corn, eating a few grains, and then attacking
another head. Where green parrots are plentiful the
long-suffering *ryot* sets them down among the ills to
which the flesh is heir. When the crops are cut the
parrots feed among the stubble, picking up the fallen
grain.

The exceedingly swift, arrow-like flight of the green
parrot is too familiar to need description. The flocks
usually fly high up, screaming loudly ; at times, however,
they skim along the ground ; occasionally they thread
their way among trees, avoiding the branches in the
most wonderful manner, considering the pace at which
they move.

Very amusing it is to watch a little company of parrots in a tree. Sometimes the birds perch on the topmost branches and there chuckle to one another; at others they cling to the trunk, looking very comic, pressed up against the bark with tails outspread. Not infrequently one sees two of them sitting together in a tree indulging in a little mild flirtation, which, in green parrot communities, takes the form of head tickling. These birds are very skilled climbers; they move along the branches foot over foot, using the beak when they have to negotiate a difficult pass. Thus they clamber about, robbing the tree of its fruit and keeping up a running conversation. Suddenly the flock will take to its wings and fly off, screeching boisterously. The members of each little community seem to live in a state of rowdy good-fellowship. No one who watches parrots in a state of nature can doubt that existence affords them plenty of pleasure.

Green parrots nest in January or February in Southern India, and somewhat later in the North. The courtship of the rose-ringed species is thus described by Captain Hutton : " At the pairing season the female becomes the most affected creature possible, twisting herself into all sorts of ridiculous postures, apparently to attract the notice of her sweetheart, and uttering a low twittering note the while, in the most approved style of flirtation, while her wings are half spread and her head kept rolling from side to side in demi-gyrations; the male sitting quietly by her side, looking on with wonder as if fairly taken aback—and wondering to see her make such a guy of herself. I have watched them during these courtships until I have felt humiliated at seeing how closely the follies of mankind resembled those of the brute creation. The only return the male made to these antics was scratching the top of her head with the point of his beak, and joining his bill to hers in a loving kiss."

Note that it is the hen that makes the advances. There can be no mistake about this, for the presence of the rose-coloured ring round the neck enables us to distinguish at a glance the cock from the hen.

The more I see of birds the more convinced do I become that, in the matter of selecting mates, the hens do not have things all their own way. In monogamous species the cock frequently chooses his spouse; selection is mutual.

The nest is a cavity in a tree, and is thus described by Hume: "The mouth of the hole, which is circular and very neatly cut and, say, two inches on the average in diameter, is sometimes in the trunk, sometimes in some large bough, and not unfrequently in the lower surface of the latter. It generally goes straight in for two to four inches, and then turns downwards for from six inches to three feet. The lower or chamber portion of the hole is never less than four or five inches in diameter, and is often a large natural hollow, three or four times these dimensions, into which the bird has cut its usual neat passage."

My experience differs from that of Hume, inasmuch as it tends to show that green parrots do not excavate their own holes, or even the entrances to them. I suppose I have seen over a hundred green parrots' nests,

o

and all have been in existing hollows. Green parrots frequently evict the squirrels which tenant a cavity in a tree and use it for nesting purposes.

They sometimes nest in holes in buildings. There is in Lahore an old half-ruined gateway, known as the *Chauburgi*. In this dozens of green parrots nest simultaneously.

The rose-ringed paroquet (*Palæornis torquatus*) seems usually to nest in trees, while the larger Alexandrine paroquet (*Palæornis nepalensis*) nests by preference in holes in buildings.

The nest hole is not lined.

Four white eggs are usually laid. Both parents take turns at incubation.

Parrots are birds which thrive remarkably well in captivity. This, I fear, is a doubtful blessing, for it leads to a vast number of the birds being taken prisoner. Many of those which are kept by natives, and even some kept by Europeans, are, I am afraid, cruelly treated. It is true that the cruelty is in many cases unintentional, but this does not afford the poor captive much consolation.

Parrot-catching is a profitable occupation in India; since nestlings fetch from four to eight annas each. Thousands of young birds are dragged out of their nurseries every year and sold in the bazaars.

Nor are the young birds immune from capture after they have left the nest. They roost for a few nights in company before dispersing themselves over the face of the country. The wily bird-catcher marks down one of these nesting spots—he has possibly had to pay rent for it, for parrot-catching is quite a profession, so large is the demand for captive birds—and then sets in likely places split pieces of bamboo smeared over with bird-lime. When daybreak comes the unlucky birds that have chanced to roost on the limed bamboos find that they cannot get away, that they are stuck to their perches!

Natives of India are very fond of taming parrots. They capture the birds at an age when they are unable to feed themselves. These young parrots are considered as members of the family, and are allowed to roam about at large in the room in which their master lives. They make a great noise and so are not very desirable pets.

I am sometimes asked by those who keep parrots how to make them talk. This is not an easy question to answer. Some birds are much more ready to learn than others. I do not consider that the various Indian species make such good talkers as some other kinds, as, for example, the West African parrot—the grey one with the red tail. Nevertheless, what follows applies indiscriminately to all species of parrot. If you want to make a bird learn quickly to talk, use plenty of bad language before it. It is really wonderful how rapidly a parrot will pick up swear words. There appears to be an incisiveness about them which appeals to parrot nature. As a rule it requires much patience to teach a parrot anything except profanity. Constant repetition of the same sound before the bird is necessary. The gramophone is said to make the best teacher. The instrument should be made to repeat slowly and steadily the phrase it is desired to teach the bird, and placed quite close to the parrot's cage, which should be covered up. A word of warning to those who try this up-to-date method of instruction. Polly's lesson should not last much longer than ten minutes, and only one a day be given; otherwise the poor bird may get brain fever.

THE ROOSTING OF THE SPARROWS

MOST species of birds like to roost in companies, partly because it is safer to do so, partly for the sake of companionship, and sometimes, in England at any rate, because by crowding together they keep each other warm. Birds have their favourite roosting places. Certain trees are patronised while others are not. Perhaps one clump will be utilised every night for a month or longer, then a move will be made to another clump. Later on a return may be made to the original site. I do not know what determines these changes of locality.

The sunset hour is, I think, the most interesting at which to watch birds. They seem to be livelier then than at any other time of the day; they are certainly more loquacious. The dormitory of the crows, the mynas, or the green parrots is a perfect pandemonium. Whilst listening to the uproar one can only suppose each member of the colony to be bubbling over with animal spirits and intent on recounting to his fellows all the doings of the day.

Most people may be inclined to think that it is impossible to derive much pleasure from observing so common a bird as the sparrow. This is a mistake. Often and often have I watched with the greatest pleasure the roosting operations of this despised bird. I know of a row of bushes that forms the dormitory of hundreds of sparrows. To enable the reader to appreciate what follows, let me say that the hedge in question is only some twenty yards long, its height is not much greater than that of a man, it is nowhere more than eight feet in breadth, and is within a hundred yards of an inhabited bungalow. Less than six yards away from it is a well, fitted with a creaking Persian wheel, at which coolies are continually working.

If you happen to pass this hedge within an hour of sunset, you will hear issuing from it the dissonance of many sparrows' voices. You stop to listen, and, as you wait, a flock of sparrows dives into the thicket. You look about to see whether any more are coming and observe nothing. Suddenly some specks appear in the air, as if spontaneously generated. In two seconds these are seen to be sparrows. Within half a minute of the time you first set eyes upon them they are already in the bushes. They are followed by another little flock of six or seven, and another and another. Flight after flight arrives in quick succession, each of which shoots into the roosting hedge. I use the word "shoot" advisedly, for no other term describes the speed at which they enter the bushes. Their flight, although so rapid, is not direct ; it takes the form of a quavering zigzag. Some of the flocks do not immediately plunge into the bushes. They circle once, twice, thrice, or even oftener, before they betake themselves to their leafy dormitory. Sometimes part of a flight dive into the hedge immediately upon arrival, while the remainder circle round and then fling themselves into the bushes as though they were soldiers performing a well-practised manœuvre; the first bird to reach the bush entering at the nearest end, the next a little farther on, the third still farther, and so on, so that the last sparrow to arrive enters the hedge at the far end. Sometimes a flock perches for a time on a tree near by before entering the hedge. Those who have only noticed sparrows pottering about will scarcely be able to believe their eyes when they see the speed at which they approach the roosting place. For the moment they are transformed into dignified birds.

All this time those individuals already in the hedge are making a great noise. Their chitter, chitter, chitter never for a moment ceases or even diminishes in intensity. Once in the hedge, the sparrows do not readily leave it. There is much motion of the leaves and branches, and birds are continually popping out of one part of the bushes into another. It is thus evident that there is considerable fighting for places. If, while all this is going on, you walk up to part of the hedge and shake it, the birds disturbed will only fly a yard or two and at once settle elsewhere in the thicket.

Meanwhile the sun has nearly set; the coolies near by have ceased working and are kindling a fire within a couple of yards of the bushes. But the sparrows appear to ignore both them and their fire. Settling down for the night engrosses their whole attention.

As the sun touches the horizon the incoming flights of sparrows become fewer and fewer; and after the golden orb has disappeared only one or two belated stragglers arrive. Sparrows are early roosters. Something approaching three thousand of them are now perched in that small hedge, yet none are visible except those that pop in and out, when jockeyed out of positions they have taken up. But although only a few sparrows come in after the sun has set, it is not until fully fifteen minutes later that there is any appreciable abatement of the din. It then becomes more spasmodic; it ceases for half a second, to burst forth again with undiminished intensity.

Twenty minutes or so after sunset the clamour becomes suddenly less. It is now possible to discern individual voices. The noise grows rapidly feebler. It almost ceases, but again becomes louder. It then nearly stops a second time. Perhaps not more than twenty voices are heard. There is yet another outburst, but the twitterers are by now very sleepy. Suddenly there is perfect silence for a few seconds, then more feeble twittering, then another silence longer than the last.

It is not yet dark, there is still a bright glow in the western sky. The periods of silence grow more prolonged and the outbursts of twittering become more faint and of shorter duration.

It is now thirty-nine minutes after the sun has set and perfect stillness reigns. The birds must have all fallen asleep. But no! one wakeful fellow commences again. He soon subsides. It has grown so dark that you can no longer see the sparrow-hawk perched on a tree hard by. He took up his position there early in the evening, and will probably breakfast first thing to-morrow morning off sparrow!

You now softly approach the bushes until your face

touches the branches.   There are twenty or thirty sparrows roosting within fifteen inches of you.   You cannot
see any of them, but if you were to stretch forth your
hand you could as likely as not catch hold of one.   You
disturb a branch and there is a rustling of a dozen pairs
of wings, so close to you that your face is fanned by the
wind they cause.   You have disturbed some birds, but
they are so sleepy that they move without uttering a
twitter.   You leave the bush and return an hour later.
Perfect silence reigns.   You may now go right up to the
roosting hedge and talk without disturbing any of the
three thousand birds.   You may even strike a match
without arousing one, so soundly do they sleep.

Those who wish to rid a locality of a superabundance
of sparrows might well profit by the fact that the birds
sleep so soundly in companies.   Could anything be
easier than to throw a large net over such a hedge and
thus secure, at one fell blow, the whole colony?

A GAY DECEIVER

THE drongo cuckoo (*Surniculus lugubris*) is a bird of which I know practically nothing. I doubt whether I have ever seen it in the flesh. It is, of course, quite unnecessary to apologise for discoursing upon a subject of which one's knowledge is admittedly *nil*. In this superficial age the most successful writers are those most ignorant of their subject. When you know only one or two facts it is quite easy to parade them properly, to set them forth to best advantage. They are so few and far between that there is no danger of their jostling one another or bewildering the reader. Then, if you are conversant only with one side of a question, you are able to lay down the law so forcibly, and the public likes having the law laid down for it, it does not mind how crude, how absurd, how impossible one's sentiments are so long as one is cocksure of them and is not afraid to say so.

My lack of knowledge of the habits of the drongo cuckoo is, however, not my chief reason for desiring to write about it. I wish to discuss the bird because natural selectionists frequently cite it as bearing striking testimony to the truth of their theory, whereas it seems to me that it does just the opposite. *Surniculus lugubris* is, so far as I am able to judge, an uncompromising opponent of those zoologists who pin their faith to the all-sufficiency of natural selection to account for evolution in the organic world.

The drongo cuckoo is as like the king-crow as one pea is to another. This bird, says Blanford, " is remarkable for its extraordinary resemblance in structure and colourisation to a drongo or king-crow (*Dicrurus*). The plumage is almost entirely black, and the tail forked owing to the lateral rectrices being turned outwards." Blanford further declares that the bird, owing to its remarkable likeness to the king-crow, is apt to be overlooked.

This being so, it is quite unnecessary for me to describe the drongo cuckoo ; it is the image of a king-crow. But stay, perhaps there are some who do not know this last bird by sight. Such should make its acquaintance. They will find it sitting on the next telegraph wire they pass—a sprightly black bird, much smaller than the crow (with which it has no connection), possessing a long, forked tail. Every now and again it makes little sallies into the air after the " circling gnat," or anything else insectivorous that presents itself. When you see such a bird you may safely bet on its being a king-crow; the off-chance of its proving a drongo cuckoo may be neglected by all but the ultra-cautious.

Not much is known of the habits of this cuckoo ; but what we do know shows that, sometimes, at any rate, it makes the king-crow act as its nursemaid. Mr. Davison saw two king-crows feeding a young *Surniculus*. The consequence is that every book on natural history trots out our friend the drongo cuckoo as an example of mimicry. The mimicry is, of course, unconscious: it is said to be the result of the action of natural selection.

King-crows are, as every one knows, exceedingly pugnacious birds; at the nesting season both cock and hen are little furies, who guard the nursery most carefully and will not allow a strange species to so much as perch in the tree in which it is placed.

It is thus obvious that the cuckoo who elects to victimise a king-crow is undertaking a "big thing," yet this is what *Surniculus* does. It accomplishes its aim by trickery; it becomes a gay deceiver, disguising itself like its dupe. Now I readily admit that the disguise may be of the utmost use to the *Surniculus*; I can well understand that natural selection will seize hold of the disguise when once it has been donned and possibly perfect it; but I cannot see how natural selection can have originated the disguise *as such*.

The drongo cuckoo may be called an ass in a lion's skin, or a lion in an ass's skin, whichever way one looks at things. When once the skin has been assumed natural selection may modify it so as better to fit the wearer; but more than this it cannot do.

I do not pretend to know the colour of the last common ancestor of all the cuckoos, but I do not believe that the colour was black. What, then, caused *Surniculus lugubris* to become black and assume a king-crow-like tail?

A black feather or two, even if coupled with some lengthening of the tail, would in no way assist the cuckoo in placing its egg in the drongo's nest. Suppose an ass were to borrow the caudal appendage of the king of the forest, pin it on behind him, and then advance among his fellows with loud brays, would any donkey of average intelligence be misled by the feeble attempt at disguise? I think not. Much less would a king-crow be deceived by a few black feathers in the plumage of a cuckoo.

I do not believe that natural selection has any direct connection with the nigritude of the drongo cuckoo. It is my opinion that, so far as the struggle for existence is concerned, it matters little to an animal what its colour be. Every creature has to be some colour : what that actual colour is must depend upon a great many factors ; among these we may name the metabolic changes that go on inside the animal, its hereditary tendencies, sexual selection, and natural selection. Is it natural selection that has caused the king-crow to be black ? I trow not.

The drongo is black because it is built that way ; its tendency is to produce black feathers. Just as some men tend to put on flesh, so also some species of birds tend to grow black plumage. In the case of the king-crow sexual selection has possibly contributed to the bird's nigritude. It is possible that black is a colour that appeals to king-crow ladies. " So neat, you know ; a bird always looks well in black, and a forked tail gives him such an air of distinction."

As the hen drongo is a bird capable of looking after herself, even when incubating, there is no necessity for her to be protectively coloured. As I have repeatedly declared, one ounce of good solid pugnacity is a better weapon in the struggle for existence than many pounds of protective colouration.

Again, in the case of king-crows nigritude may be an expression of vigour, the outward and visible sign of strength.

Let me make myself clear. Suppose that in a race of savages those that had fair hair were stronger, bolder, more prolific, and more pushing than the dark-haired men. Fair hair, in some inexplicable way, always accompanied strength and the like. It is obvious that, under these conditions, the race would in time become fair-haired: the milder dark men would eventually be hustled out of existence. Fair hair would then be the outward expression of vigour: it would not be the cause of vigour, merely the accompaniment of it; nor would it be a direct product of natural selection. In the same way it is possible that among drongos nigritude is in some manner correlated with vigour. This idea is not altogether fanciful. Are there not horses of "bad colour"? Are not white "socks" a sign of weakness? Is not roan a colour indicative of strength and endurance in a horse?

May not the blackness and the forked tail of the drongo cuckoo have arisen in the same way as they arose in the king-crow? In each case it may be an accompaniment of vigour, or it may be the result of sexual selection. Mrs. Surniculus may have had similar tastes to Mrs. Dicrurus, and, since cuckoos seem to be very plastic birds, her tastes have been gratified. As another example of this plasticity I may cite

Centropus phasianus—a cuckoo which is a very fair imitation of a pheasant.

On this view the resemblance is a mere chance one. The cuckoo is not an ass in a lion's skin, but an ass that looks very like a lion. His lion-like shape was not forced upon him by natural selection. A variety of causes probably contributed to it. It was not until the resemblance had arisen and become very striking that it was directly affected by natural selection.

I am far from saying that the above is a correct explanation of the nigritude: it is all pure hypothesis. Even if it be correct, we are really very little further than we were before towards an explanation of the colours and shape of either the king-crow or the drongo cuckoo.

Why did these birds tend to grow black feathers rather than red, green, or blue ones?

This is a question which "stumps" us all.

THE EMERALD MEROPS

IF I have a favourite bird it is the little green bee-eater (*Merops viridis*). There is no winged thing more beautiful or more alluring. More showy birds exist, more striking, more gorgeous, more magnificent creatures. With such the bee-eater does not compete. Its beauty is of another order. It is that of the moon rather than of the sun, of the violet rather than of the rose. The exquisite shades of its plumage cannot be fully appreciated unless minutely inspected. Every feather is a triumph of colouring. No description can do the bird justice. To say that its general hue is the fresh, soft green of grass in England after an April shower, that the head is covered with burnished gold, that the tail is tinted with olive, that a black collarette adorns the breast, that the bill is black, that a streak of that colour runs from the base of the beak, backwards, through the eye, which is fiery red, that the feathers below this streak are of the purest turquoise-blue, as are the feathers of the throat—to say all this is to convey no idea of the hundred shades of these colours, or the manner in which they harmonise and pass one into another. Nor is it easy for words to do justice to the shape of the bird ; even a photograph fails to express the elegance of its carriage and the perfection of its proportions. Were I to string together all the superlatives that I know, I should scarcely convey an adequate impression of the grace of its movements. I can but try to make the bird recognisable, so that the reader may see its beauties for himself.

He should look out for a little green bird with a black beak, slender and curved, and a tail of which the two middle feathers are very attenuated and project a couple of inches as two black bristles beyond the other caudal feathers. The bird should be looked for on a telegraph wire or the bare branch of a tree, for the habits of bee-eaters are those of fly-catchers. The larger species prey upon bees, hence the popular name, but I doubt whether the little *Merops viridis* tackles an insect so large as a bee. It feeds upon smaller flying things, which it captures on the wing. As it rests on its perch its bright eyes are always on the look out for passing insects. When one comes into view, the bird sallies forth. Very beautiful is it as it sails on outstretched wings. The under surface of these is reddish bronze, so that their possessor seems to become alternately green and gold as the sun's rays fall on the upper or lower surface of its pinions. Its long mandibles close upon its prey with a snap sufficiently loud to be audible from a distance of five or six yards. This one may frequently hear, for bee-eaters are not shy birds. They will permit a human being to approach quite near to them, as though they knew that the fulness of their beauty was apparent only on close inspection.

P

The little green bee-eater utters what Jerdon calls "a rather pleasant rolling whistling note," which, if it cannot be dignified by the name of song, adds considerably to the general attractiveness of the bird. Bee-eaters are, alas! not very abundant in Madras, but, if looked for, may be seen on most days in winter. The Adyar Club grounds seem to be their favourite resort. When driving into the club at sunset I have often surprised a little company of them taking a dust bath in the middle of the road. The bath over, the little creatures take to their wings and enjoy a final flight before retiring for the night.

Bee-eaters are, I think, migratory birds. It is true that they are found all the year round in many parts of India, but such places appear to be the winter quarters of some individuals and the summer residences of others. There is an exodus of bee-eaters from Calcutta about March. A similar event occurs in Madras, although in the latter place the birds are seen all the year round, a few remaining to breed. In Lahore, on the other hand, the birds arrive in March, and, having reared their young, leave in September.

The nest is a circular hole excavated by the bird, usually in a sandbank, sometimes in a mud partition between two fields. I saw a nest in Lahore in one of the artificial bunkers on the golf links. Major C. T. Bingham states that in 1873, when the musketry instruction of his regiment was being carried on at Allahabad, he observed several nest holes of this species in the face of the butts. The birds seemed utterly regardless of the bullets that every now and then buried themselves with a loud thud in the earth close beside them. Colonel Butler gives an account of a bee-eater nesting in an artificial mudbank, about a foot high, that marked the limits of the badminton court in the Artillery Mess compound at Deesa. One of the birds invariably sat upon the badminton net when people were not playing, and at other times on a tree close by, while its mate was sitting on the eggs. As I have already said, bee-eaters are not afflicted with shyness.

Very soon after their arrival at Lahore the birds begin their courtship. At this period they seem to spend the major portion of the day in executing circular flights in the air. They shoot forth from their perch and rapidly ascend by flapping their wings, then they sail for a little on outstretched pinions and thus return to the perch.

Courtship soon gives place to the more serious business of nest construction. When a suitable spot has been found, the birds at once begin excavating, digging away at the earth with pick-like bill and holding on to the wall of the bank by their sharp claws until the hole they are making becomes sufficiently deep to afford a foothold. As the excavation grows deeper the bird throws backwards with its feet the sand it has loosened with its beak, sending it in little clouds out of the mouth of the hole. While one bird is at work its mate perches close by and gives vent to its twittering note. After working for about two minutes the bird has a rest and its partner takes a turn at excavation. Thus the work proceeds apace. Bee-eaters look spick and span, even when in the midst of this hard labour. The dry sand that envelops them, far from soiling their plumage, acts as a dust bath. When the hole, which is about two inches in diameter, has reached a length of some four feet, it is widened out into a circular chamber about twice the size of a cricket ball. In this three or four white eggs are laid. These have been well described as " little polished alabaster balls." They are placed on the bare ground. Young bee-eaters lack the elongated bristle-like tail feathers of the adult birds. A very pleasing sight is that of a number of the youngsters sitting in a row on a telegraph wire receiving instruction in flying.

In conclusion, mention must be made of a near relative of the little bee-eater. I allude to the blue-tailed species (*Merops philippinus*), which also occurs in Madras. This is a larger and less beautiful edition of the green bee-eater. It is distinguishable by its size, the rusty colour of its throat, and its blue tail. It is usually found near water. He who shoots snipe in the paddy near Madras comes across numbers of these birds sitting on the low walls that divide up the fields. The habits of the blue-tailed bee-eater are those of its smaller cousin. Although its song is more powerful, it is a less attractive bird.

DO ANIMALS THINK?

MR. JOHN BURROUGHS contributed some time ago to *Harper's Magazine* an article bearing the above title. The leading American naturalist is so weighty an authority that I feel chary about controverting any statement made by him; but I cannot believe that he is right when he boldly asserts that animals never think at all. I agree with Mr. Burroughs when he says "we are apt to speak of the lower animals in terms that we apply to our own kind." There is undoubtedly a general tendency to give animals credit for much greater intelligence, far more considerable powers of reasoning, than they actually possess; in short, to put an anthropomorphic interpretation on their actions.

But it seems to me that Mr. Burroughs rushes to the other extreme. To deny to animals the power of thought is surely as opposed to facts as to credit them with almost human powers of reasoning. Says Mr. Burroughs: "Animals act with a certain grade of intelligence in the presence of things, but they carry away no concepts of those things as a man does, because they have no language. How could a crow tell his fellows of some future event or of some experience of the day? How could he tell them this thing is dangerous save by his actions in the presence of those things? Or how tell of a newly found food supply save by flying eagerly to it?"

Even if we admit that a crow is not able to recount the experiences of the day to his companion, it does not follow that the crow does not remember them, or cannot picture them in his mind. With regard to the last question, I have frequently seen a crow, at the sight of some food thrown out to him, caw loudly, and his friends, on hearing his cry, at once fly to the food.

Of course it is open to any one to assert that, in this case, the crow that discovers the food does not consciously call its companions; at the sight of its food it instinctively caws, and its companions obey the caw instinctively, without knowing why they do so. No one, however, who watches crows for long can help believing that they think. The fact that they hang about the kitchen every day at the time the cook pitches out the leavings seems inconsistent with the theory that birds cannot think. The crows obtained food at this place yesterday and the day before at a certain hour, and the fact that they are all on the look out for food to-day shows, not only that they possess a good memory, but that they are endowed with a certain amount of reasoning power.

Many animals have very good memories. Now, in order that an animal may remember a thing it must think. Its thoughts are of course not clothed in language as human thoughts are, but they nevertheless exist as mental pictures.

According to Professor Thorndike, the psychic life of

an animal is "most like what we feel when our con-sciousness contains little thought about anything, when we feel the sense impressions in their first intention, so to speak, when we feel our own body and the impulses we give to it (or that outward objects give to it). Sometimes one gets this animal consciousness; while in swimming, for example. One feels the water, the sky, the birds above, but with no thoughts about them, or memories of how they looked at other times, or æsthetic judgments about their beauty. One feels no 'ideas' about what movements he will make, but feels himself make them, feels his body throughout. Self-consciousness dies away. The meanings and values and connections of things die away. One feels sense-im-pressions, has impulses, feels the movements he makes; that is all."

This is probably a good description of the state of mind of a dog when he is basking in the sunlight; he is thinking of nothing. But he hears the shrill cry of a squirrel—this at once recalls to him the image of the little rodent and past *shikar*. In a moment the dog is on the alert; he is now thinking of the squirrel, and his instinct and inclinations teach him to give chase to it. Or he hears a footstep; he recognises it as that of his master, sees that the latter is wearing a *topi*, and at once pictures up a run in the compound with his master. But his owner chains him up. The dog looks wistfully at his master's retreating figure and pulls at his chain; it is surely absurd to say that the dog is not thinking. The picture of a scamper beside his master rises up before him, and he feels sad because he knows that the scamper is not likely to become a *fait accompli*.

Again, you have been accustomed to throw a stick for your dog to run after and carry back to you. You are out walking accompanied by your dog; he espies a stick lying on the ground; at once images of previous enjoyable runs after the stick rise up in his mind; he picks up the stick and brings it to you, drops it at your feet and looks up at you. You pretend to take no notice. The dog then picks up the stick and rubs it against your legs. To believe that the dog while acting thus does not think, that he is merely obeying an inborn instinct, is surely a misinterpretation of facts. Animals have but limited reasoning powers, and their thoughts are not our thoughts, they are not clothed in language, they are merely mental pictures, called up either subjectively, as when a dog barks while dreaming, or objectively by some sight or scent, but nevertheless such sensations are thoughts.

While maintaining that the higher animals can and do think, I am ready to admit that a great many of their actions which are apparently guided by reason are in reality purely instinctive. Thus the building of a nest by a bird must, at any rate on the first occasion, be a purely instinctive action. The creature cannot know what it is doing. Nor can it have any thoughts on the matter; it suddenly becomes an automaton, a machine, acting thoughtlessly and instinctively.

Some internal force which is irresistible compels it to seek twigs and weave them into a nest. The bird has no time to stop and think what it is doing, nor does it wish to, for it enjoys nest building. It is, of course, impossible for a human being to understand the frame of mind of a bird when building its first nest. The only approach to it that we ever experience is when we are suddenly seized with an impulse to do something un- usual, and we obey the impulse and are afterwards surprised at ourselves.

There is a story told of a wealthy man who had been out hunting and was returning home tired and thirsty. He dismounted at a farm-house, went inside and asked for a drink. While this was being obtained he noticed a lot of valuable old china on the dresser : seized by a sudden impulse, he knocked it all down, piece by piece, with his riding whip. His hostess on her return with the drink looked surprised. The hunting man smiled, asked her to name the value she set on the china, sat down and, there and then, wrote out a cheque for the amount.

It always seems to me that when a bird begins for the first time to collect materials for a nest she must act impulsively, without thinking what she is doing. Just as the hunting man was seized with a sudden desire to smash the crockery with his whip, so is she suddenly impelled to collect twigs and build a nest.

Another instinctive act which is apparently purpose- ful is the feigning of injury by a parent bird when an enemy approaches its young. Superficial observation of this action leads the observer to imagine that the mother bird behaves thus with deliberate intent to deceive, that in so doing she consciously endeavours to distract attention while her young ones are betaking themselves to cover. As a matter of fact, the bird will behave in precisely the same way if she have eggs instead of young ones. This has, of course, the effect of drawing attention to the eggs, and proves that the action is instinctive and not the result of reasoning.

Most people have remarked the cautious manner in which many birds approach the nest when they are aware that they are being watched. This has the appearance of a highly intelligent act. It is, however, nothing of the kind.

I have taken young birds from a nest, handled them and replaced them in full view of their frantic parents. Then I have retired a short distance and watched the parents. These invariably display the same caution in approaching the nest as they did before I had discovered its whereabouts.

Birds and beasts think much less than they are popularly supposed to do. It is absurd to attribute to them reasoning powers similar to those enjoyed by man ; it is equally absurd to assert that they do not think at all.

A COUPLE OF NEGLECTED
CRAFTSMEN

TWO Indian birds have a world-wide reputation. Every one has heard of the weaver bird (*Ploceus baya*) and the tailor-bird (*Orthotomus sutorius*). Their wonderful nests are depicted in every popular treatise on ornithology. They are both master-craftsmen and deserve their reputation. But there are in India birds who build similar nests whose very names are unknown to the great majority of Anglo-Indians. The Indian wren-warbler (*Prinia inornata*) weaves a nest quite as skilfully as the famous weaver bird. This neglected craftsman is common in nearly all parts of India, and, if you speak of the weaver bird to domiciled Europeans, they will think you mean this wren-warbler, for among such he is universally called the weaver bird; the famous weaver, whose portrait appears in every popular bird book, is known to them as the baya.

As its name implies, *Prinia inornata* is a plainly attired little bird. Its upper parts are earthy brown. It has the faintest suspicion of a white eyebrow, and its under plumage is yellowish white, the thighs being darker than the abdomen. Picture a slenderly built wren with a tail three inches in length, which looks as

though it were about to fall out and which is constantly
being waggled, and you have a fair idea of the appearance of this little weaver. But this description applies
to dozens of other birds found in India. The various
warblers are so similar to one another in appearance
as to drive ornithologists to despair. The inimitable
" Eha " admits that they baffle him. " There is nothing
about them," he writes, "to catch the imagination of the
historian, and they will never be famous. I have been
perplexed as to how to deal with them. . . . To attempt
to describe each species is out of the question, for there
are many, and they are mostly so like each other that
even the title ornithologist does not qualify one to
distinguish them with certainty at a distance. If you
can distinguish them with certainty when you have
them in your hand you will fully deserve the title."

It is, however, possible to recognise the Indian wren-
warbler by its note. When once you have learned this
you are able to identify the bird directly it opens its
mouth. But how shall I describe it? It is a peculiar,
harsh but plaintive, *twee, twee, twee ;* each *twee* follows
close upon the preceding one, and gives you the idea
that the bird is both excited and worried. If you see a
fussy little bird constantly flitting about in a cornfield
and uttering this note, you may be tolerably certain
that the bird is the Indian wren-warbler. It never rises
high in the air ; it is but an indifferent exponent of the
art of flying. It moves by means of laborious jerks of
its wings. It is a true friend to the husbandman, since
it feeds exclusively on insects. The most remarkable
thing about it is its nest. This is a beautifully woven

structure, composed exclusively of grass or strips of leaves of monocotyledonous plants which the bird tears off with its bill. These strands are invariably very narrow, and are sometimes less than one-twentieth of an inch in breadth. The nest may be described as an egg-shaped purse, some five or six inches in depth and three in width, with an entrance at one side, near the top. It is devoid of any lining, and its texture puts one in mind of a loosely made loofah. The nest is sometimes attached to two or more stalks of corn, or more commonly it is found among the long grasses which are so abundant in India. When the nest is built in a cornfield the birds have to bring up their family against time. They are unable to begin nest-building until the corn is fairly high, and must, if the young are to be safely started in life, have brought them to the stage when they are able to leave the nest by the time the crop is cut.

In India nearly every field of ripe corn has its family of wren-warblers; the two parents flit about, followed by a struggling family of four. These little birds do not by any means always defeat time. Numbers of their nests containing half-fledged young are mown down at every harvest by the reaper's sickle. The nest is woven in a manner similar to that adopted by the baya; the cock and hen in each case work in combination. Its texture is looser than that of the more famous weaver, but it is not less neatly put together. In it are deposited four or five pretty little green eggs, marked with brown blotches and wavy lines.

Our second neglected craftsman is a tailor. It sews

a nest so like that of the world-famous tailor as to be almost indistinguishable from it. Some authorities declare that the two nests are distinguishable. They assert that the nest of *Orthotomus* is invariably lined with some soft substance, such as cotton-wool, the silky down of the cotton tree, soft horse-hair, or even human hair, while that of the species of which we are speaking is lined with grass or roots. This distinction does not, however, invariably hold. I have seen nests of this species which have been lined with cotton-wool.

This bird is known to ornithologists as the ashy wren-warbler (*Prinia socialis*). Anglo-Indian boys call it the tom-tit. It is a dark ashy-grey bird, with the sides of the head and neck and the whole of the lower plumage buff. There is a tinge of rufous in the wings and tail. It is most easily distinguished by the loud snapping noise it makes during flight. How this noise is produced we do not know for certain. Reid was of opinion that the bird snapped its long tail. What exactly this means I do not know. Jesse believes that the sound is produced by the bird's mandibles. I have spent much time in watching the bird, and am inclined to think that the noise is caused by the beating of the wings against the tail. This last is constantly being wagged and jerked, and it seems to me that the wings beat against it as the bird flits about. When doves and pigeons fly, their wings frequently meet, causing a flapping sound. I am of opinion that something similar occurs when the ashy wren-warbler takes to its wings.

Perhaps the most extraordinary thing about this bird is the well-authenticated fact that it builds two types of nest. Besides this tailor-made nest, the species makes one of grass, beautifully and closely woven, domed, and with the entrance near the top. I have never seen this latter type of nest, but so many ornithologists have that there can be no doubt of its existence.

The strange thing is that both types of nest have been found in the same neighbourhood, so that the difference in the form of nursery is not a local peculiarity.

I am at a loss to account for the existence of these two types of nest. I have no idea how the habit can have arisen, nor do I know what, if any, benefit the species derives from this peculiarity. So far as I am aware, no one can say what it is that leads to the construction of one type of nest in preference to the other. The nests of this species present a most interesting ornithological problem. I hope one day to be in a position to throw some light on it; meanwhile I shall welcome the news that some one has forestalled me. The ashy wren-warbler is a common bird, so that most Anglo-Indians have a chance of investigating the mystery. The same kind of eggs are found in each type of nest. They are of exceptional beauty, being a deep mahogany or brick-red, so highly polished as to look as though they have been varnished.

BIRDS IN THEIR NESTS

J UST as every Englishman is of opinion that his
house is his castle, so does every little bird resent
all attempts at prying into its private affairs in
the nest. For this reason we really know very
little of the home-life of birds. It is not that there are
no seekers after such knowledge. Practical ornithology
is a science that can boast of a very large number of
devotees.

Many men spend the greater part of their life in
endeavouring to wrest from birds some of their secrets,
and such must admit that the results they obtain are as
a rule totally disproportionate to the magnitude of the
efforts. At present we know only the vague generalities
of bird life.

We know that the hen lays eggs; that she, with or
without the help of the cock, as the case may be, in-
cubates these eggs; that the young, which are at first
naked, are fed and brooded until they are ready to
leave the nest, when they are coaxed forth by the
parents, who hold out tempting morsels of food to them.
But these are mere generalities. Our ignorance of de-
tails is very great.

The nests of most passerine birds are scrupulously clean.
Young birds have enormous appetites, and much of the

food which they eat is indigestible and must pass out as droppings, yet in the case of many species no sign of these droppings is visible, either in the nest, or on the leaves, branches, or the ground near the nest. What becomes of these droppings? Ornithological treatises are silent upon this subject.

Again, young birds are born naked, and in India are frequently exposed to very high temperatures, so that much liquid must pass from their bodies by evaporation. How is this liquid made good? Do the parents water the birds, if so, how? I have never seen any mention of this in an ornithological treatise.

Let us to-day consider these two subjects : the sanitation of the nest and the method of assuaging the thirst of young nestlings.

As regards the first we have some knowledge, thanks to the patient labours of Mr. F. H. Herrick, an American naturalist, whose book, *The Home Life of Birds*, I commend to every lover of the feathered folk. Unfortunately, Mr. Herrick's book is to some extent spoiled for Englishmen, because it deals with birds with which they are unfamiliar ; nevertheless, its general results apply to all passerine birds.

Mr. Herrick is a very keen bird photographer. As every one knows, he who wishes to obtain good photographs of birds has two great difficulties to overcome. The first is to get near to his subjects, and the second is to find them and their nests in situations suitable for photography.

The former is usually overcome by the photographer concealing himself and his camera in a tent or other

Q

structure. At first the birds are afraid of the concealing object, but soon maternal affection overcomes their fear.

Mr. Herrick's method of overcoming the second of these two difficulties is to remove the nest to be photographed from the concealed situation in which it is usually built, and place it in a more open place. If the nest be thus moved when the young are some seven or eight days old, the parents will almost invariably continue to feed their young in the new situation, for at that particular period the parental instinct is at its zenith. In addition to obtaining a splendid series of photographs, Mr. Herrick has observed, from a distance of a few inches, the nesting habits of several American birds. As the result of these observations he is able to declare that nest-cleaning follows each feeding with clock-like regularity. " The excreta of the young," he writes, " leave the cloaca in the form of white opaque or transparent mucous sacs. The sac is probably secreted at the lower end of the alimentary canal, and is sufficiently consistent to admit of being picked up without soiling bill or fingers. The parent birds often leave the nest hurriedly bearing one of these small white packages in bill, an action full of significance to every member of the family. . . . Removing the excreta piecemeal and dropping it at a safe distance is the common instinctive method, not only of insuring the sanitary condition of the nest itself, but, what is even more important, of keeping the grass and leaves below free from any sign which might betray them to an enemy." These packets of excrement are quite odourless, and they are often devoured by the parent bird instead of being carried away. The digestion of very young birds must be feeble, and doubtless much of the food given them passes undigested through the alimentary canal, so that it is capable of affording nourishment to the parents. Birds are nothing if not economical.

Of course, all birds are not so careful of the sanitation of the nest. Every one knows what a filthy spectacle a heronry is. According to Mr. Herrick, the instinct of inspecting and cleaning the nest is mainly confined to the great passerine and picarian orders. It is obviously not necessary in the case of those birds, such as fowls, of which the young are able to run about when born; nor is it needful in the case of birds of prey, who take no pains to conceal the whereabouts of the nest. Young raptores eject their semi-fluid excreta over the edge of the nursery; thus the nest is kept clean, but the droppings on the ground betray its presence to all the world.

Coming now to our other question: How do young birds obtain the water which they require? we have no help from Mr. Herrick. He makes no mention of this in his most interesting book. It is possible that nestlings are not given anything to drink, that the juicy, succulent insects or fruits with which they are supplied contain sufficient moisture for their requirements. We must remember that the skin of birds is very different from that of man. It contains no sweat glands, so that a bird, like a dog, can only perspire through its mouth.

The breath of mammals is so surcharged with moisture that when it is suddenly cooled the water vapour in it condenses; the result is we can "see the breath" of a mammal on a cold day. I have never succeeded in seeing a bird's breath, so am of opinion that the fowls of the air do not exhale so much moisture as mammals do. But even allowing for this, a considerable amount of moisture must be given out in expiration, so that it seems probable that young birds require more moisture than they obtain in their food. Drops of water have to be administered to hand-reared birds. Many birds fill up the crop with food and then discharge the contents into the gaping mouths of their young. In this condition the food must be mixed with a considerable quantity of saliva and possibly with water. The crop of a bird is a receptacle into which the food passes and remains until actually utilised. There seems no reason why water should not be stored for a short time in this receptacle just as food is. Perhaps birds " bring up " water as they do solid food, and thus assuage the thirst of their young. Such a process would be very difficult to detect; it would be indistinguishable from ordinary feeding to the casual observer. I hope that some physiologist will take up the matter. A quantitative analysis of the air exhaled by a bird should not be very difficult to make.

BULBULS

MORE than fifty species of bulbul are found in India—bulbuls of all sorts and conditions, of all shapes and sizes, from the brilliant green bulbuls (which, by the way, strictly speaking, are not bulbuls at all) to the dull-plumaged but blithe white-browed member of the community, so common in Madras; from the rowdy black bulbuls of the Himalayas to the highly respectable and well-behaved red-vented bulbuls. He who would write of them is thus confronted with an *embarras de richesses*. The problem that he has to solve is, which of the many species to take as his theme.

The polity of birds is said to be a republic. The problem may, therefore, well be elucidated on democratic principles. The first and foremost of these—the main plank of every demagogue's platform—is, of course, "one bulbul, one vote." The second is like unto the first, "every bulbul for itself." Therefore, on being asked to elect a representative to be the subject-matter of this paper, each will vote for his own species, and the result of the poll will be: Bulbuls of the genus *Molpastes* first, those of the genus *Otocompsa* a good second, and the rest a long way behind. Let us then conform to the will of the majority and consider for a little these two species of bulbul, which resemble one another very closely in their habits.

Molpastes is a bird about half as big again as the sparrow, but with a longer tail. The whole head is black and marked by a short crest. There is a conspicuous crimson patch of feathers under the tail. The remainder of the plumage is brown, but each feather on the body is margined with creamy white, so that the bird is marked by a pattern that is, as " Eha " points out, not unlike the scales on a fish. Both ends of the tail feathers are whitish.

Otocompsa is a more showy bird. The crest is long and projects forward over the forehead. The crimson patch, so characteristic of bulbuls, also exists in this species. There is a similar patch on each side of the head—whence the bird's name, the red-whiskered bulbul. There is also a white patch on each cheek. The white throat is separated from the whitish abdomen by a conspicuous dark brown necklace. This bird must be familiar to every one who has visited Coonoor or any other southern hill station. The less showy variety—the red-vented bulbul, as it is called— is common in and about Madras.

It will be noticed that I have refrained from giving any specific name to either of these two genera. This is due to the fact that these bulbuls are widely distributed and fall into a number of local races, each of which has some little peculiarity in colouring. For this reason, bulbuls are birds after the heart of the museum ornithologist. They afford him ample scope for species-making.

THE BENGAL RED-WHISKERED BULBUL. (OTOCOMPSA EMERIA)

If you go from Madras to the Punjab you will there meet with a bulbul which you will take for the same species as the bulbul you left behind in Madras. But if you look up the birds in an ornithological text-book you will find that they belong to different species. The Punjab bulbul is known as *Molpastes intermedius*, while the Madras bird is called *M. hæmorrhous*. The only difference in appearance between the two species is that in the Madras bird the black of the head does not extend to the neck, whereas in the Punjab bird it does. Similarly, there is a Burmese, a Tenasserim, a Chinese, and a Bengal red-vented bulbul.

Now, I regard all these different bulbuls as local races of one species, which might perhaps be called *Molpastes indicus ;* and I think that I am justified in holding this view by the fact that the bulbuls you come across at Lucknow do not fit in with the description of any of these so-called species. The reason is that the Bengal and the Madras races meet at Lucknow, and of course interbreed. The result is a cross between the two races.

In addition to the above there are some *Molpastes* which have white cheeks and a yellow patch under the tail. In all, nine or ten Indian "species" of *Molpastes* have been described.

The same applies in a lesser degree to *Otocompsa*. This is a widely distributed species, but is not so plastic as *Molpastes*. There is the Bengal red-whiskered bulbul (*Otocompsa emeria*), which is distinguishable from the southern variety (*O. fuscicaudata*) by having white tips to the tail feathers, and the dark necklace interrupted in the middle. There is also an *Otocompsa* with a yellow patch under the tail.

This division of a species or genus into a number of races or nearly allied species is interesting as showing one of the ways in which new species arise in Nature quite independently of natural selection. It is unreasonable to suppose that the extension into the neck of the black of the head in the Punjab bulbul and its non-extension in the Madras bulbul are due to the action of natural selection in each locality, that a bulbul with black in its neck is unfitted for existence in Madras.

Whenever a group of animals becomes isolated from its fellows, it almost invariably develops peculiarities which are of no help to it in the struggle for existence. Thus isolation is the cause of the origin of dialects and languages. A dialect is an incipient language, even as a race is a potential species.

But let us return to our bulbuls. The habits of both *Otocompsa* and *Molpastes* are so similar that we can speak of them together. They are what Mr. Finn calls thoroughly nice birds. They are, none of them, great songsters, but all continually give forth exceedingly cheery notes. The twittering of the red-whiskered bulbuls is not the least of the charms of our southern hill stations.

Bulbuls feed on insects and berries, so are apt to be destructive in gardens. They built nests of the orthodox type—cups of the description always depicted on Christmas cards. These are built anywhere, without much attempt at concealment. Rose bushes are a favourite site, so are crotons, especially if they be in a verandah. A pair of bulbuls once built a nest in my greenhouse at Gonda. Among the fronds of a fern growing in a hanging basket did those unsophisticated birds construct that nest. Every time the fern was watered the sitting bird, nest, and eggs received a shower-bath!

Sometimes bulbuls do by chance construct their nest in a well-concealed spot, but then they invariably " give the show away " by setting up a tremendous cackling whenever a human being happens to pass by.

I have had the opportunity of watching closely the nesting operations of seven pairs of bulbuls; of these only one couple succeeded in raising their brood. The first of these nests was built in a croton plant in a verandah at Fyzabad. One day a lizard passed by and sucked the eggs. The next was the nest at Gonda already mentioned. In spite of the numerous waterings they received, the eggs actually yielded young bulbuls; but these disappeared when about four days old. The *mali* probably caused them to be gathered unto their fathers. The third nest was situated in a bush outside the drawing-room window of the house in which I spent a month's leave at Coonoor. This little nursery was so well concealed that I expected the parents would succeed in rearing their young. But one morning I saw on the gravel path near the nest a number of tell-tale feathers. Puss had eaten mamma bulbul for breakfast! The fourth nest—but why should I detail these tragedies? Notwithstanding all their nesting disasters, bulbuls flourish so greatly as to severely shake one's faith in the doctrine of natural selection.

In conclusion, a word or two must be said concerning bulbuls in captivity. These birds make charming pets, but as their diet is largely insectivorous, they cannot be fed on seed. They become delightfully tame. One I kept used to fly on to my shoulder whenever it saw me, and open its mouth, flutter its wings, and twitter, which was its way of asking to be fed. It *would* insist on using my pen as a perch, and as one's handwriting is not improved by an excitable bulbul hopping up and down the penholder, I was obliged to shut the bird up in a cage when I wanted to write. The bulbul used to resent this, and did not hesitate to tell me so. In young birds the tail is very short, and the patch of feathers under it is pale red instead of being bright crimson.

Natives of India keep bulbuls for fighting purposes. These birds are not caged, but are tied to a cloth-covered perch by a long piece of fine twine attached to the leg. Bulbuls, although full of pluck, are not by nature quarrelsome. In order to make them fight they are kept without food for some time. Then two ravenous birds are shown the same piece of food. This, of course, leads to a fight, for a hungry bulbul is an angry bulbul.

THE INDIAN CORBY

I HAVE never been able to discover why the great black crow (*Corvus macrorhynchus*), so common in India, is called the jungle-crow. It is, indeed, true that the corby is found in the jungle, but it is found everywhere else in most parts of India, and is certainly abundant in villages and towns, being in some places quite as much a house bird as its smaller cousin, the grey-necked crow.

Considering the character of the larger species and its extensive distribution, one hears remarkably little about it. The explanation is, of course, that the house-crow absorbs all the attention that man has to bestow upon the sable-plumaged tribe. The prevailing opinion seems to be that the black crow is merely a mild edition, a feeble imitation of, a scoundrel of lesser calibre than, its smaller cousin, *Corvus splendens*, and, therefore, everything that applies to the house-crow applies in a lesser degree to the big-billed bird. This is, I submit, a mistaken view, the result of imperfect observation. *Corvus macrorhynchus* has an individuality of his own, and we do him scant justice in dismissing him with a short paragraph at the foot of a lengthy description of *Corvus splendens*.

In saying this, I feel that I am speaking as one having

authority, and not as the Scribes and Pharisees, whose zoological horizon coincides with the limits of the museum. For a period of eighteen months I lived in a station which should be renamed and called Crowborough. To assert that the place in question swarms with crows is, of course, to assert nothing, for it shares this feature with every other place in India. The point I desire to bring out clearly is that in this particular place the black crows are nearly as numerous as the grey-necked birds. The former are certainly in a minority, but their minority is, like Sir Henry Campbell-Bannerman's in the previous House of Commons, a large one, and what they lack in numbers they make up in weight and beak-force. It was truly delightful to watch them lord it over the grey-necked birds. Grammarians will observe that I here use the past tense. This is a point of some importance. Just as it is impossible to properly estimate the character of an eminent man during his lifetime, so is it to form a proper opinion of the personality and behaviour of a species of crow while one is in the midst of that species, while one is subjected to the persecutions, the annoyances, and the insults to which it thinks fit to treat one.

But I am now far away from Crowborough, and I may never again return thither. As I sit upon the Irish shore and see the blue waters of the North Atlantic roll softly up against the black rocks of Antrim, I feel that I am in a position to form a true estimate of the character of *Corvus macrorhynchus*.

Until I went to Crowborough I laboured under the

delusion that the grey-necked crow knew not the meaning of the word " respect." The deference with which the big-beaked species is treated by his smaller cousin came as a complete surprise to me.

Most Anglo-Indians are so embittered against the whole tribe of the *corvi* that they will on no account feed them. I do not share this prejudice. I am able to see things from the corvine point of view. Were I a crow I should most certainly consider man fair game.

While in Crowborough I invariably gave the surplus of my *tiffin* to the crows. Those in the locality of my office window did not take long to find this out. The grey-necked crows were the first to make the discovery. It takes these less time to put two and two together than it does the more sluggish-brained black crows. At the end of a few days quite half-a-dozen grey-necked fellows had learned to hang about my windows at the luncheon hour. They used to sit in a row along each window-ledge. One day a corby appeared upon the scene. His arrival was the signal for the departure of his grey-necked brethren. From that day onwards he regarded that ledge as his special preserve, and whenever a house-crow ventured on to the ledge he " went for " it savagely with his great beak. The intruder never waited long enough to enable him to get a blow home. Thus the hunting-ground of the grey-necked crows became restricted to one of the window-ledges.

In order to tease the black fellow I used sometimes to throw all the food to the window in which the grey crows were perched. He would fly round and drive them off that ledge and then give me a bit of his mind !

Later on he introduced his wife. She took possession of one window and he of the other; so that the poor house-crows no longer had " a look in." Some of the bolder spirits among them used certainly to settle on the shutters in hopes of catching a stray crumb, but none durst venture on to the ledge while a black crow was there.

Upon one occasion I put a whole milk pudding upon the ledge ; the corbies would not allow the house-crows so much as a peck at the dainty dish until they themselves had had their fill.

Every one knows that the grey-necked crows, when harassing a creature more powerful than themselves, work in concert. It is my belief that two of these birds acting together are more than a match for any other creature. The way in which a pair of them will, by alternate feint and attack, take food away from a great kite or a dog is truly admirable. But so great is the respect of the grey-necked crows for the corby that I have never seen them attack him in this way. This says volumes for the force of character of *Corvus macrorhynchus*. He is quite an Oliver Cromwell among birds. He is a dour, austere, masterful, selfish bird— a bird which it is impossible to like or to despise.

When he has once made up his mind to do anything there is no deterring him from the accomplishment thereof. Early in the year one of these birds spent at least the greater part of a day in trying to secure for its nest one of the twigs in a little circular fence erected for the protection of a young tree. The fence in question was composed of leafless branches, interlaced and tied together. One of these twigs, being loose at one end, was pounced upon by a black crow who intended to carry it to his or her nest. But the other end was securely fastened. I watched that crow at intervals for several hours. Whenever I looked it was grappling in vain with the refractory twig. The work was, it is true, frequently interrupted, for natives kept passing by. But immediately the human being had gone, the crow resumed the attack. Every now and again it would fly to a dust-bin hard by and alight on the rim in order to take a breather. Occasionally it would dive into that bin in order to secure the wherewithal to feed the inner crow. It would then return to work like a giant refreshed.

I am of opinion that that dust-bin was to the crow what the public-house is to the British working man.

APPENDIX

1. *Corvus corax.* The Raven.
2. *Corvus corone.* The Carrion Crow.
3. *Corvus frugilegus.* The Rook.
4. *Corvus cornix.* The Hooded Crow.
5. *Corvus monedula.* The Jackdaw.
6. *Graculus eremita.* The Red-billed Chough.
7. *Pyrrhocorax alpinus.* The Yellow-billed Chough.
8. *Pica rustica.* The Magpie.
9. *Regulus cristatus.* The Goldcrest.
10. *Lanius collurio.* The Red-backed Shrike.
11. *Ampelis garrulus.* The Waxwing.
12. *Oriolus galbula.* The Golden Oriole.
13. *Pastor roseus.* The Rose-coloured Starling.
14. *Siphia parva.* The European Red-breasted Flycatcher.
15. *Muscicapa grisola.* The Spotted Flycatcher.
16. *Geocichla sibirica.* The Siberian Ground Thrush.
17. *Monticola saxatilis.* The Rock Thrush.
18. *Saxicola aenanthe.* The Wheatear.
19. *Cyanecula wolfi.* The White-spotted Bluethroat.
20. *Turdus viscivorus.* The Missel Thrush.
21. *Turdus pilaris.* The Fieldfare.
22. *Turdus iliacus.* The Redwing.
23. *Linota cannabina.* The Linnet.

24. *Passer montanus.* The Tree Sparrow.
25. *Passer domesticus.* The House Sparrow.
26. *Emberiza schoeniclus.* The Reed Bunting.
27. *Emberiza pusilla.* The Dwarf Bunting.
28. *Emberiza hortulana.* The Ortolan Bunting.
29. *Emberiza melanocephala.* The Black-headed Bunting
30. *Fringilla montifringilla.* The Brambling.
31. *Alauda arvensis.* The Skylark.
32. *Calandrella brachydactyla.* The Short-toed Lark.
33. *Galerita cristata.* The Crested Lark.
34. *Anthus trivialis.* The Tree Pipit.
35. *Anthus richardi.* Richard's Pipit.
36. *Anthus campestris.* The Tawny Pipit.
37. *Anthus spinoletta.* The Water Pipit.
38. *Anthus pratensis.* The Meadow Pipit.
39. *Hirundo rustica.* The Swallow.
40. *Cotile riparia.* The Sand Martin.
41. *Chelidon urbica.* The Martin.
42. *Motacilla alba.* The White Wagtail.
43. *Motacilla melanope.* The Grey Wagtail.
44. *Motacilla borealis.* The Grey-headed Wagtail.
45. *Motacilla flava.* The Blue-headed Wagtail.
46. *Iynx torquilla.* The Wryneck.
47. *Merops phillippinus.* The Blue-tailed Bee-eater.
48. *Merops apiaster.* The European Bee-eater.
49. *Upupa epops.* The Hoopoe.
50. *Coracias garrula.* The European Roller.
51. *Cypselus alpinus.* The Alpine Swift.
52. *Cypselus apus.* The European Swift.
53. *Caprimulgus europaeus.* The European Nightjar.
54. *Strix flammea.* The Barn Owl.
55. *Scops giu.* The Scops Owl.
56. *Asio otus.* The Long-eared Owl.

57. *Asio accipitrinus*. The Short-eared Owl.
58. *Bubo ignavus*. The Eagle Owl.
59. *Nyctea scandiaca*. The Snowy Owl.
60. *Alcedo ispida*. The Common Kingfisher.
61. *Cuculus canorus*. The Cuckoo.
62. *Gyps fulvus*. The Griffon Vulture.
63. *Neophron percnopterus*. The Egyptian Vulture.
64. *Milvus migrans*. The Black Kite.
65. *Haliaetus albicilla*. The White-tailed Sea Eagle.
66. *Pandion haliaetus*. The Osprey.
67. *Accipiter nisus*. The Sparrow Hawk.
68. *Astur palumbarius*. The Goshawk.
69. *Aquila chrysaetus*. The Golden Eagle.
70. *Aquila maculata*. The Large Spotted Eagle.
71. *Buteo desertorum*. The Common Buzzard.
72. *Circus cineraceus*. Montagu's Harrier.
73. *Circus cyaneus*. The Hen Harrier.
74. *Circus aeruginosus*. The Marsh Harrier.
75. *Elanus caeruleus*. The Black-winged Kite.
76. *Falco peregrinus*. The Peregrine Falcon.
77. *Falco subbuteo*. The Hobby.
78. *Aesalon regulus*. The Merlin.
79. *Tinnunculus alaudaris*. The Kestrel.
80. *Tinnunculus cenchris*. The Lesser Kestrel.
81. *Columbia livia*. The Blue Rock Pigeon.
82. *Turtur communis*. The Turtle Dove.
83. *Coturnix communis*. The Quail.
84. *Rallus aquaticus*. The Water-Rail.
85. *Crex pratensis*. The Corn Crake.
86. *Porzana parva*. The Little Crake.
87. *Porzana maruetta*. The Spotted Crake.
88. *Fulica atra*. The Coot.
89. *Gallinula chloropus*. The Moorhen.

90. *Grus communis.* The Crane.
91. *Anthropoides virgo.* The Demoiselle Crane.
92. *Otis tarda.* The Great Bustard.
93. *Otis tetrax.* The Little Bustard.
94. *Oedicnemus scolopa.* The Stone Curlew.
95. *Glareola pratincola.* The Pratincole.
96. *Cursorius gallicus.* The Cream-coloured Courser.
97. *Strepsilas interpres.* The Turnstone.
98. *Charadrius fulvus.* The Eastern Golden Plover.
99. *Charadrius pluvialis.* The Golden Plover.
100. *Vanellus vulgaris.* The Lapwing.
101. *Squatarola helvitica.* The Grey Plover.
102. *Aegialitis alexandrina.* The Kentish Plover.
103. *Aegialitis dubia.* The Little Ringed Plover.
104. *Aegialitis hiaticula.* The Ringed Plover.
105. *Haematopus ostralegus.* The Oystercatcher.
106. *Himantopus candidus.* The Black-winged Stilt.
107. *Limosa belgica.* The Black-tailed Godwit.
108. *Limosa lapponica.* The Bar-tailed Godwit.
109. *Numenius arquata.* The Curlew.
110. *Numenius phaeopus.* The Whimbrel.
111. *Recurvirostra avocetta.* The Avocet.
112. *Totanus hypoleucus.* The Common Sandpiper.
113. *Totanus glareola.* The Wood Sandpiper.
114. *Totanus ochropus.* The Green Sandpiper.
115. *Totanus callidus.* The Redshank.
116. *Totanus fuscus.* The Spotted Redshank.
117. *Totanus glottis.* The Greenshank.
118. *Tringa minuta.* The Little Stint.
119. *Tringa temmincki.* Temminck's Stint.
120. *Tringa subarquata.* The Curlew Stint.
121. *Tringa alpina.* The Dunlin.
122. *Tringa platyrhyncha.* The Broad-billed Stint.

123. *Calidris arenaria.* The Sanderling.
124. *Pavoncella pugnax.* The Ruff.
125. *Phalaropus hyperboreus.* The Red-necked Phalarope.
126. *Phalaropus fulicarius.* The Grey Phalarope.
127. *Scolopax rusticula.* The Woodcock.
128. *Gallinago coelestis.* The Common Snipe.
129. *Gallinago gallinula.* The Jack Snipe.
130. *Larus ichthyaetus.* The Great Black-billed Gull.
131. *Larus ridibundus.* The Laughing Gull.
132. *Larus affinis.* The Dark-backed Herring Gull.
133. *Hydrochelidon hybrida.* The Whiskered Tern.
134. *Hydrochelidon leucoptera.* The White-winged Black Tern.
135. *Sterna angelica.* The Gull-billed Tern.
136. *Sterna cantiaca.* The Sandwich Tern.
137. *Sterna fluviatilis.* The Common Tern.
138. *Sterna dougalli.* The Roseate Tern.
139. *Sterna minuta.* The Little Tern.
140. *Sterna fuliginosa.* The Sooty Tern.
141. *Hydroprogne caspia.* The Caspian Tern.
142. *Stercorarius crepidatus.* Richardson's Skua.
143. *Stercorarius pomatorhinus.* The Pomatorhine Skua.
144. *Oceanites oceanicus.* Wilson's Petrel.
145. *Anous stolidus.* The Noddy.
146. *Phalacrocorax carbo.* The Cormorant.
147. *Platalea leucorodia.* The Spoonbill.
148. *Nycticorax griseus.* The Night Heron.
149. *Ardea manillensis.* The Purple Heron.
150. *Ardea cinerea.* The Common Heron.
151. *Herodias alba.* The Large Egret.
152. *Herodias garzetta.* The Little Egret.
153. *Bulbulcus coromandus.* The Cattle Egret.
154. *Ardetta minuta.* The Little Bittern.

155. *Ciconia alba.* The White Stork.
156. *Ciconia nigra.* The Black Stork.
157. *Plegadis falcinellus.* The Glossy Ibis.
158. *Phoenicopterus roseus.* The Flamingo.
159. *Cygnus olor.* The Mute Swan.
160. *Cygnus musicus.* The Whooper.
161. *Anser ferus.* The Grey-lag Goose.
162. *Anser albifrons.* The White-fronted Goose.
163. *Anser erythropus.* The Lesser White-fronted Goose.
164. *Anser brachyrhynchus.* The Pink-footed Goose.
165. *Tadorna cornuta.* The Sheld-Duck.
166. *Casarca rutila.* The Brahminy Duck.
167. *Mareca penelope.* The Widgeon.
168. *Anas boscas.* The Mallard.
169. *Chaulelasmus streperus.* The Gadwall.
170. *Nyroca ferruginea.* The White-eyed Duck.
171. *Nyroca ferina.* The Pochard.
172. *Nyroca marila.* The Scaup.
173. *Nyroca fuligula.* The Tufted Duck.
174. *Netta rufina.* The Red-crested Pochard.
175. *Dafila acuta.* The Pintail.
176. *Clangula glaucion.* The Golden-Eye.
177. *Spatula clypeata.* The Shoveller.
178. *Querquedula urcia.* The Garganey Teal.
179. *Nettium crecca.* The Common Teal.
180. *Podiceps cristatus.* The Great Crested Grebe.
181. *Podiceps nigricollis.* The Eared Grebe.
182. *Mergus albellus.* The Smew.
183. *Merganser castor.* The Goosander.
184. *Merganser serrator.* The Red-breasted Merganser.

GLOSSARY

Babul. *Acacia arabica.* A thorny tree.

Badmash. A bad character, a ruffian.

Barsath. Rain.

Bhabar. The waterless tract of forest-clad land between the Himalayas and the *Terai.* It is from ten to fifteen miles in breadth and higher than the general level of the plains.

Chaprassi. Lit. a badgeman. A servant who runs messages, an orderly.

Chik. A number of thin pieces of bamboo strung together to form a curtain. Thin chiks are usually hung in front of doors in India with the object of keeping out flies but not air. Chiks of stouter make are hung from the verandah in order to keep out the sun.

Chit. Short for *Chitti,* a letter or testimonial.

Coolie. An unskilled labourer.

Dhak. *Butea frondosa.* A common tree in low jungle.

Dhobi. Washerman.

Dirzie. Tailor.

Farash. *Tamarix indica.*

Gali galoj. Abuse.

Jhil. A lake, broad tank, or any natural depression which is filled with rain water at certain seasons or permanently.

Kankar, or Kunkar. Lumps of limestone with which roads are metalled in Northern India.

Kannaut. The sides of a tent.

247

Khansamah. Cook.

Khud. A deep valley.

Mali. Gardener.

Murghi. Barndoor Fowl.

Neem. *Azadirachta melia,* a common tree in India.

Paddy. Growing rice.

Puggarree. A turban.

Ryot. A cultivator, small farmer.

Sal. The iron-wood tree (*Shorea robusta*).

Sahib. Master, sir, gentleman; a term used to denote a European.

Shikar. Hunting or shooting.

Shikari. (1) The man who goes hunting or shooting.
  (2) The native who accompanies him and directs the beat.

Terai. Lit. "Moist land." A marshy tract of land about twelve miles broad, between the *Bhabar* and the plains proper. It is low-lying.

Tiffin. Lunch.

Topi. A sun-helmet.

With the exception of *British Birds in the Plains of India*, which appeared in *The Civil and Military Gazette*, and *The Indian Corby, Birds in the Rain*, and *Do Animals Think?* which came out in *The Times of India*, the articles which compose this book made their *debût* in one or other of the following papers: *The Madras Mail, The Indian Field, The Englishman.*

The author takes this opportunity of thanking the editors of the above-named newspapers for permission to reproduce these essays.

R 2

INDEX

INDEX

253